AF531568

Differential Childhood

About the Authors

Dr. Shankar Das is an Associate Professor in the School of Health System Studies, Tata Institute of Social Sciences (A Deemed University), Mumbai, India. He has been associated with many reputed organizations as a resource person such as the Department of Atomic Energy, GOI, NPCIL, BSES, Unilever, NOCIL, Larsen and Toubro, Tata Memorial Hospital and Sir JJ Group of Hospitals and Grant Medical College. Also, he is Consultant to many government and non-governmental organizations in India and abroad. In 2004 he was Technical Consultant to the World Health Organization to upscale and develop behavioural health component in the Union of Myanmar. Dr. Das has directed over fifteen Action Research Projects on various psychosocial and behavioural aspects, in the field of health, training technology, counselling, reproductive health and HIV/AIDS. He has to his credit many research works published in various reputed journals and books.

Ms. Ashima Das is a Senior Research Fellow and pursuing doctoral studies at the Tata Institute of Social Sciences. She has been working in the field of correctional and health social work since the last seven years. She has extensively worked with children and adults with disabilities in educational and community settings. Currently she is freelance consultant to various NGOs and CBOs working in the field of health and development. Ms. Das has participated and presented several papers in various national and international conferences.

DIFFERENTIAL CHILDHOOD

Shankar Das
Ashima Das

CONCEPT PUBLISHING COMPANY PVT. LTD.,
NEW DELHI-110059

ISBN: 13-978-81-8069-670-1

First Published 2010

Published and Printed by

Concept Publishing Company Pvt. Ltd.
Regd. Office:
A/15-16, Commercial Block, Mohan Garden
New Delhi-110059 (India)
Phones : 25351460, 25351794, *Fax* : 091-11-25357109
Email : publishing@conceptpub.com,
Website: www.conceptpub.com

Editorial Office:
H-13, Bali Nagar, New Delhi-110 015, India.

Cataloging in Publication Data-- *Courtesy:* D.K. Agencies (P) Ltd. <docinfo@dkagencies.com>

Das, Shankar.
Differential childhood / Shankar Das, Ashima Das.
p. cm.
Includes bibliographical references.
Includes index.
ISBN 13: 9788180696701 ISBN 10: 8180696707

1. Children with disabilities--Family relationships. 2. Children with disabilities--Civil rights. 3. Children with disabilities--Civil rights--India. 4. Children with disabilities--Education. 5. Children with disabilities--Education--India. 6. Inclusive education. 7. Inclusive education--India. 8. Child development. I. Das, Ashima, joint author. II. Title.

DDC 305.9080954 22

PREFACE

This work aims to study the developmental perspectives and educational initiatives for children with disabilities. This study comprise five research chapters which have been carefully drafted for getting a holistic understanding of the ecological systems as they exist and influence the education of the children with disabilities. Lerner (1993), in terms of child development, described the "goodness of fit" which referred to the match between the developmental needs of children and the demands, resources and capacities of their family, school and community environments. Children adapt to specific demands and expectations from home, school and community as part of the developmental process. The attitudes, values, expectations and stereotypes other people have about how a child should be, or act, mould the child. The skills and competencies required of a child by home, school and community, also shape development. A child's behaviour in the face of these demands will depend on his or her skills, resources, support and experiences. It is important to understand that these systems are interdependent and interacting and change at one level may also affect the other systemic layers. For example, if we propose inclusive education for children with disabilities it requires action at two levels - the school level and the systems level. The school level action calls for changes in classroom organization, resource utilization, curriculum modification and the systems level changes require parental and community support, legislations, societal views on inclusion etc.

The forthcoming five chapters have been planned and written to understand and address the abovementioned issues. The chapters have been sequenced in a manner to get a comprehensive understanding of the systemic layers (See Figure 1.0). The child's development is seen as occurring within several nested personal, familial, social and cultural contexts. The outermost mesosystemic layer depicts the wider framework within which the inner layers of agencies, school, community, family and child operate. The next few layers narrow into the community, the family influencing and interacting with the child.

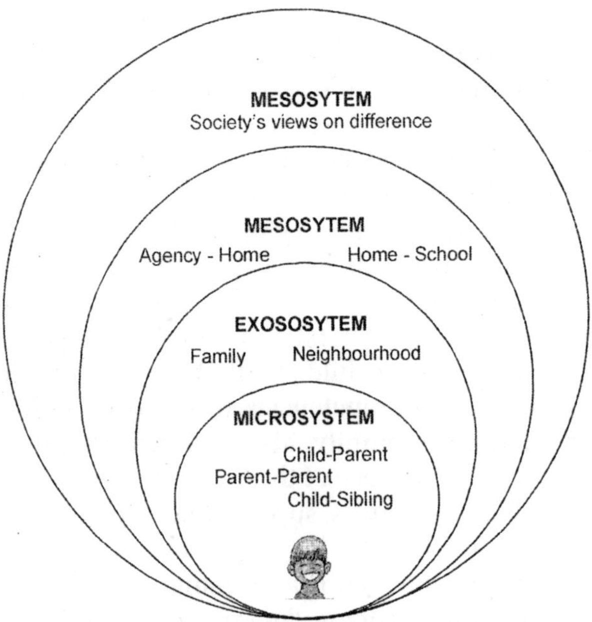

Fig. 1.0: *Development Contexts as related to Educational Initiatives*

The chapters dealing with conceptualization of disability and rights of children with disabilities fall within an understanding of the macro influences and implications on child's development and his/her education. The chapter on psychosocial responses of the families leads to a theoretical comprehension of the familial coping and response to a child with special needs. Lastly, the two chapters explore the philosophy, perspectives and initiatives of inclusion and its exemplification in the high income countries. A layout of the chapters has been given below to provide a rationale, scope and overview of each chapter.

The first chapter titled 'Understanding Disability' helps the audience to develop complete understanding of disability. The chapter is an attempt to develop a comprehensive understanding and gaining a conceptual clarity on disability. The chapter reviews the existing models and explanations of disabilities. There is a greater amount of emphasis on the social construction of disability. The social model looks at disability as a representation of the diversity of human experience. The aim of the chapter is to see the potential impact of the social model of disability on programmes and policies for the individuals with disabilities.

The chapter endeavours to discuss the different paradigms on disability constructs. It looks at the existing models within the three key paradigms; the impairment perspective, the functional perspective and the ecological perspective. It attempts to trace how these models evolved through the activism and struggle of the population with disabilities. It also tries to see the relevance of these models in designing services and programmes for the people with disabilities in Indian context.

The second chapter is titled 'Children with Special Needs: Family Responses.' Most imperative functions of the family are to rear and educate children so that they prepared to be independent, self-sufficient and productive in the society. A child's behaviour and thought reflects his parenting and family environment. Family assumes a greater importance when the child has some special needs to which it needs to cater. There are a number of research studies on responses of families to the special needs of the children. It was, therefore, considered vital to understand these family processes which affect the personality of the child and his/her development. The chapter is a theoretical exploration of the psychosocial responses of families of children with special needs. The chapter reviews four family models which have guided research in this area.

The chapter is an elucidation of various family theories which have guided the researches on psychosocial responses of families having children with special needs. The section following the explanation of the theory contextualizes it to the families of the children with special needs. The final segment of the chapter endeavours to compare and critique the models and concludes with the reflection of the learning from these on the intervention arena.

The third chapter is on 'Rights of Children with Disability'. Disability must be understood within the context of human rights. Children with disabilities have long been discriminated against their normally developing peers, hence denying them equal opportunities in all spheres. The Convention on the Rights of the Child has been ratified by most countries in the world but the provisions are largely being ignored with reference to the children with disabilities. There are serious violations reported from across the globe. For a child with disability, the violation may be in comparison to the treatment of others in the community or family, e.g. all children in the family go to school except the child with a disability. Thus, it makes it vital to study the rights to which the children with disability are entitled. The chapter analyses the provisions of the Convention on the Rights of the Child, in light of the prevailing situation in India.

The chapter looks at the development of a rights based approach in disability. It examines the provisions of the Convention on the Rights of the Child (CRC) *vis-à-vis* its translation in Indian context. The concluding section attempts a discussion on the reasons for the present situation and looks at advocacy as a tool for change.

The fourth chapter is titled 'Inclusive Education'. Children with disabilities are one of the most disadvantaged groups in our society. In addition to their perceptible physical and circumstantial limitations they are subjected to innumerable ways of social discrimination, impoverished education and reduced work opportunities. They are undeniably the victims of inequity, marginalization and of a vicious cycle of multiple deprivation. Society in very subtle ways further disables the person by labelling and exclusion. Philosophically, there is a movement towards a more inclusive society that does not separate and segregate individuals based on the differences that are often misunderstood. Understanding these positive, newer trends in the field of education hence, becomes crucial.

The chapter attempts to look at the philosophy, perspectives and initiatives for inclusive education in international and national context. There is an endeavour to elucidate the meaning and implication of inclusive education for all learners. The chapter discusses some requisites in inclusive education that illustrate how to strengthen processes of inclusion in school settings.

The chapter consists of five major segments. The first section discusses the philosophy of inclusion. The following section looks at inclusive education and special education comparatively. The subsequent sections explore international and country initiatives in the field of inclusive education. The final segment delves into the practical necessities of inclusion process with some concluding observations and remarks.

The last chapter elucidates 'Inclusive Education - Lessons from High Income Nations'. The idea of 'normalization' was developed in Scandinavia in the 1960s. It aimed towards providing a pattern of life as normal as possible. Normalization implied that almost all disabled people would live in the community, participate in the normal activities and relationships experiencing choices, and having full access to social and educational opportunities. Amongst other landmark developments in the field of education of children with special needs is the Warnock Committee Report, UK, 1978 which highlighted the importance of educating children in their crucial years and placed education of children with disabilities amongst its top priorities. An initiative in a similar direction in USA was made by launching of "Head Start", an education programme by President Lyndon Johnson in 1964. The most unique characteristic of the programme was that it admitted children with disabilities as well. The high income nations have led the battle against the discrimination of disabled children and contributed a great deal in development of the global statutes. It was therefore essential to develop a comprehensive knowledge base of the current developments in the developed nations on education of children with disabilities for developing a comprehensive understanding of inclusive education.

The chapter looks at policies and programmes for education of the children with special needs in United Kingdom and United States of America. It examines the policy provisions and action initiatives in the field of education of children with special needs in United Kingdom and United States of America. A comparative analysis follows the detailed discussion of the policies and programmes of the two nations.

Note : The use of phrase "children with disabilities" represents the authors' belief that a child with a disability is a child first who has differential abilities. At some places, the phrase "children with special needs" was used interchangeably. The authors acknowledge that the latter is a much broader concept and would encompass children other than having a disability as well. Nonetheless, the terminology was used because the international documents and the present legislations in some countries are using this phrase. Therefore, the authors express this concern at the outset and requests the audience to consider the two terms transposable for this book.

Reference

Lerner, J. (1993). The Influence of Child Temperamental Characteristics on Parent Behaviours. In Luster, T. Okagaki, L. (Eds.), *Parenting: An Ecological Perspective*. Hillsdale, New Jersey: Lawrence Erlbaum Associates.

ACKNOWLEDGEMENTS

A book requires intelligence, diligence, patience, assistance and blessings. We have been fortunate to have got this opportunity to present our thoughts and ideas for wider audience. Our initial thanks are reserved for our revered deity. Like always, we would thank Him at the outset for making this voyage a smooth one.

Our sincere gratitude to Prof. S. Parasuraman, Director, Tata Institute of Social Sciences for creating an enabling environment for everyone to pursue their academic interests. We are indebted to the Institute for the excellent infrastructural support it has provided which has facilitated our writing. We would especially like to thank the Library, which not only provided a physical space for us to work but also contributed in terms of sharing the unlimited resources to which there was an open access. The staff deserves a special mention for giving all the necessary support; issuing books, journal access, fetching inter-library loans and retrieving books on demands.

It is hard to achieve goals unless the person gets full hearted support from his/her family. We thank our wonderful parents, Babu, Maa, Kaku and Mummy, for their blessings and best wishes. We would also take this opportunity to thank all our family members and friends who were confident of our ability and perseverance for accomplishing this task.

Shankar Das
Ashima Das

CONTENTS

1

UNDERSTANDING DISABILITY

Introduction

The issues about defining and conceptualizing disability and how persons with disabilities perceive themselves are knotty and complex. It is no coincidence that these questions are emerging at the same time when the status of persons with disabilities in society is changing dramatically. The cause of some of these changes is activism by the people with disabilities, as well as the result of the corresponding shift in international policy.

It is indeed a challenge to conceptualise a term which is complicated and multidimensional. There have been attempts from different disciplines to do so accomplishing a definitive purpose. Whether the focus of a definition was impairment, disability or handicap, all the explanations have touched on some significant facet. There is however no single definition or model that encompasses the varied aspects of disability.

The chapter entirely takes a theoretical standpoint. It endeavours to present the diverse viewpoints of various disciplines. It may be noted that these viewpoints have emerged in a chronological sequence. Any conceptualization would be affected by the sociological, economical, political and historical context. As there was a movement from extermination to segregation to inclusion the definitions of disability have also undergone changes.

The model explanations of disability were developed by the disabled activists in the West in order to give shape to the changing ideology. The best possible explanation of disability and its related concepts came from the social model, clearly because it was developed by the disabled people themselves. It transcends the belief system of regarding the disabilities as medical deficits which require medical intervention or societal intervention in the form of charity. The social model describes the disablement process of an individual by the society and promotes the principle of equalization of opportunities. The chapter therefore, endeavours to explicate these concepts so as to arrive at an understanding of disability and see how it has affected the public opinion and policy.

Evolution of the Concept of Disability

The awareness about the fact that it is undemocratic practice by the able-bodied people to make important decisions concerning lives of the disabled people did not come until the disabled people raised their voices against the age-old discrimination and segregation. The writings by the disabled people have revealed how they have struggled for their basic citizenship rights in institutions as well as communities.

In the 1950s, many parents, friends and other interested people realized that the disabled young people needed services, such as specialized education services and activities to occupy themselves and lead a productive life. Many organizations which were established belonged to the non-profit sector working for field prevention of disability and the integration of disabled people into the society. All of these organisations were 'unidisability', i.e. focused on a single disability. Some organizations made concerted efforts to incorporate disabled people themselves in the membership, let alone the decision making functions of the organizations (Dreidgar, 1989).

Social Death Model

Miller and Gwynne (1972) in their research conducted in Le Court Cheshire Home, London wherein they described the disabled people as socially dead, dependent on others for a 'cure' or to provide permanent 'care'. Inadvertently, the struggles of the residents of Cheshire Home were an attempt towards social characterization of disability. This construction was called the 'social death model of disability' by Finkelstein (1991). The publication by Miller and Gwynne might have added clarity to the reasons behind public attitudes it however did not encourage the residents of the Cheshire Home to welcome the better management of their 'social death'.

Towards Organizing Power

It was until 1965, when two disabled women founded the Disablement Income Group (DIG) which though expressed wide concerns for social rights, had the dominant focus on the campaign of disability allowance. It did provide an excellent forum to the disabled people to come together at the grassroots level. This approach however was not promoted by other disabled activists especially Paul Hunt, who had led the movement within the Cheshire Home. According to him by asking compensations for their disabilities, they were reinforcing the belief that disability results in inability to function socially, which in turn encourages the dependency of disabled people on special provisions and concessions by the able-bodied people, which precisely was the situation the residents had endeavoured to change. He believed that the real issue was getting submerged under the single issue campaigns in response to statutory provisions. He wanted an approach which could give the disabled a better status and recognition in the society.

He gave a call to all like-minded people through his article in the national newspaper. He received an overwhelming response from many active disabled people who felt in the similar way. After a year long intense discussion regarding an adequate approach to address disability issues, a new organization called the "Union of the Physically Impaired Against Segregation" (UPIAS) was founded.

Theories from Action

The action guidelines of UPIAS were based on social oppression theory of disability and the inherent model could be termed as "social barriers model of disability" (Finkelstein 1991:25). Initially, UPIAS attracted only the most active but gradually the social construction of disability percolated to the disabled community. Another organization, Liberation Network of the People with Disabilities (LNPD), which was also set up in the early 1970s, promoted the same ideology. The two organizations upheld the social oppression of disabled people and caused a greater drift from DIG. On the other side, a group branched out from DIG, which advocated effective pressure on government for a disability income. They named themselves Disability Alliance. This led to further weakening of DIG. Thus, it is evident that there was no unified approach towards disability issues and concerns. This brought the UPIAS and Disability Alliance to a meeting where they were to reach a consensus regarding fundamental meaning of disability and appropriate way forward. They were unable to reach to any agreement but a Report entitled, "Fundamental Principles of Disability" was released in 1976. UPIAS expanded its policy statement in this document by attempting to clearly define disability in social terms. Based on this contention, they proposed the problems related to disability could be solved only when disabled people were involved in decision-making. The Disability Alliance however maintained that disability is associated with poverty and it is poverty, which needs to be tackled first with State Disability Allowance before disabled people could participate at the helm of affairs. This definition suggested that a disabled individual was intrinsically non-equal to their peers and required their help. Both the groups talked about social deprivation, whereas UPIAS believed in social and environmental barriers to be the cause, Disability Alliance saw it as a result of personal inadequacy. Because of the difference in their fundamental belief system regarding causes of social deprivation of disabled individual, their approaches to action were also different. While Disability Alliance encouraged campaign for state relief urging the Government to provide special services to compensate for their disabilities, UPIAS searched for new ways to empower the disabled community so that they could engage in changing the society by eliminating the barriers that were seen disabling. UPIAS upheld that it is the society which is organized in such a way so as to ignore the disabled individual which brings about their "social death". The intervention choices were therefore reduced to either cure the individual condition or provide elaborate system of care. Unfortunately, both these intervention strategies assumed that disability is an individual's problem. These approaches involved the imposition of able-bodied standards of normality when defining appropriate actions on behalf of disabled people. This laid the foundation of the administrative model of disability, which assumed services could be "delivered in the separate, but tightly linked, cure and care areas of intervention." Each of these forms of service provision was, of course, guided by their own subset of the administrative model. For disabled people these were the rehabilitation and personal care service models. Rehabilitation services were prescribed on the well known medical model and personal care services on the imperfectly identified welfare model of disability. Both these models of disability should be regarded as sub-sets of the dominant "social death model of disability" (Finkelstein, 1991:27).

The Renaissance

The situation continued and led to complete marginalisation of the disabled population. It was not until 1970s when the disabled struggled for greater power over their own lives which provided the experience of challenging the prevailing understanding of disability and development of their own interpretation of the situation. This paved way to the growth of the new social theory of disability and a firm argument on right to exercise control over their own affairs and support services. Logically, this view advocated for service approaches, which focus on barrier removal. An approach to disability where all people are regarded as equal, problems in personal achievement are attributed to social and personal barriers that restrict or disable their potential rather than to the limitations imposed by their deficits, is an outcome of the revolution where the people with disabilities came together to fight for their rights. The people with disabilities in the United Kingdom, United States of America and certain European countries spearheaded the battle for their rights as equal individuals.

The disability studies have emerged as an academic discipline owing to the activism and experiences of people with disabilities. "Most of the definitions of disability frequently found in scholarly research are actually models made up of several concepts that have either directed or reciprocal relationships with one another" (Altman, 2001:100). A closer look at the existing models would help us understand the diversity and intricacy of the subject.

The Disability Models

It is difficult to point out the number of models which exist as different disciplines have their own perspectives on disability. All the models, however, could be classified under broad categories which help to understand the various conceptualizations that have been attempted.

Oliver (1983) originally conceptualized models of disability as the binary distinction between what he chose to call the individual and social models of disability. He borrowed the idea of the individual and the social model from the distinction originally made between impairment and disability by the Union of the Physically Impaired against Segregation in 1976. Oliver (1990 a) made a clear distinction between the individual and social models of disabilities and endeavoured to place the other prevailing models within the two expansive frameworks. He contended that there are two fundamental points about the model which are noteworthy. Firstly, it locates the 'problem' of disability within the individual and secondly, it sees the causes of this problem as stemming from the functional limitations or psychological losses which are assumed to arise from disability.

The genesis, development and articulation of the social model of disability by disabled people themselves were a rejection of all of these fundamentals (Oliver, 1990 b). It did not rule out the existence of the problem but located it in the society. It is not individual limitations, of whatever kind, which are the cause of the problem but society's failure to provide appropriate services and adequately ensure the needs of disabled people are fully taken into account in its social organisation. Though he located the medical model of disability within the individual model, he considered it incomplete and inappropriate. The logic behind his contention was that disability is a social state and not just a medical condition. Hence medical intervention in, and more importantly, control over disability is inappropriate. Doctors are trained to diagnose, treat and cure illnesses, not to alleviate social conditions or circumstances. His powerful argument was that the doctors too often think themselves as experts and know-all and thus, believe that they have the cure for everything. According to Oliver, disability itself is a life long social condition without a medical cure; the illnesses associated with it may however require treatment.

Having a disability does not necessarily require a medical intervention which would be targeted towards achieving normalcy. The quandary here is the normal standards that have been set for everything and the disabled individuals are seen as deviants who require treatment for their inability.

Table 1.1 summarizes the three key classification systems and related models and their interpretations and definitions of disability. The models related to the first two perspectives shown in the table define disability primarily as a fixed medical condition or impairment with no or limited consideration for the socioeconomic or cultural context. By emphasizing the limitations of abilities as a result of an impairment or disability, these models follow an exclusionary approach. Models related to the ecological perspective shift towards a more integrative approach that prioritizes situational and contextual aspects in their definition of disability.

The impairment perspective considers disability a health problem or abnormality that is situated in an individual's body or mind. The medical model, which views disability in terms of disease, illness, abnormality and personal tragedy, best expresses this perspective. It focuses on impairment and considers disability a health problem or abnormality that is situated in an individual's body or mind. The medical model assumes that disability as an intrinsic characteristic of individuals with disabilities. This has serious practice implications as it attempts to cure the individuals' abnormalities and defects, which are seen as strictly personal conditions. The medical model was an offshoot of the development in the modern medicine in the 19th century, which enhanced the role of the physician in the society. The rationale that goes behind it, disabilities are believed to have medical origins, the disabled individuals were supposed to benefit under the directions of the medical

Table 1.1 : Key Classification Systems and Related Models

Impairment Perspective	Functional Perspective	Limitation	Ecological Perspective
Definition or interpretation of disability	Disability is considered a health problem or abnormality that is situated in an individual's body or mind	Disability is directly caused by impairment and defined primarily by medical criteria. In contrast to medical model, consideration is given to the social and physical environment	Disability is the result of an interaction of impairment, activity limitations, and participation restrictions in a specific social or physical environment.
Relevant models	Medical model–Disability is classified or interpreted by disease, illness, abnormality.	Nagi model – Disability is defined by characteristics of impairment and the situational context.	Quebec disability production process model – Disability is the result of the interaction of personal factors (e.g., age, gender), environmental factors or social context, and life habits (e.g. person's aily activities).

Contd . . .

Table 1.1 : contd...

Impairment Perspective	Functional Perspective	Limitation	Ecological Perspective
	International Classification of Diseases (ICD) – Coding system focusing on diseases and health conditions a revised and updated by the World Health Organization (WHO)	International Classification of Impairments, Disabilities and Handicaps (ICIDH) – First classification system focusing solely on disability. Developed by the WHO. Disability is defined by the reduction or lack of ability, caused by impairment, to perform an activity in a way considered normal for a human being.	The social model – Disability is primarily interpreted as society's failure to acknowledge and accommodate the needs of persons with disabilities rather than a medical condition. Human-rights model – Disability is defined as a social construct focusing on individuals' human rights and dignity International Classification of Functioning, Disability and Health – Revision of ICIDH. Disability is defined as the intraction between impairment and externally imposed activity limitations or participation restrictions.

Source : Human Resources Development, Canada (HRDC), "Defining Disability: A Complex Issue," Cat. No.: RH37-4/3-003E (Gatineau, Quebec: HRDC, 2003), 6-7. Cited in Groschl, 2005.

professionals. The individual was considered the originator and bearer of the problem. In short, the medical specialists could provide the solution to the problem of disability. The society has no obligation towards the disabled population in terms of adapting to their diverse needs.

The individual with a disability assumes a sick role under the medical model. Just like the societal obligations are relaxed for sick individuals, even the disabled people are not expected to fulfil those normal roles like attending school, taking up a job, having a family of their own etc. They are expected to yield authority to the medical professionals whom they require to get better. The medical model as is evident is very narrow in focus. It locates the problem within the individual and proposed only a medicinal cure.

Until recently, the effect of the medical model was seen in most of the policy issues and programmes which concentrate mainly on health, thus placing the authority in the medical professionals. What fits well within this impairment paradigm is the International Classification of Diseases (ICD), which is a system of coding diseases and health conditions that is used by most health services around the world. The World Health Organization (WHO), the body responsible for periodically revising the ICD, released the tenth revision (ICD-10) in 1999. The ICD was developed exclusively in consultation with international medical and rehabilitation professionals, including associations of hospitals and medical doctors; it did not involve persons with disabilities or their organizations. The ICD also remains silent on the social and environmental aspects of impairment and disability.

The functional limitations perspective arose from attempts to expand the medical model to include non-medical criteria of disability, especially the social and physical environment. Nevertheless, the notion that impairments were the direct cause of disability remained central to this perspective. Also, like the impairment perspective, the functional limitations perspective considered disability in quantitative terms, measuring functional restrictions against a standard. Under the Nagi model (Nagi, 1965: 100-13) functional limitations are a distinct concept. The limitations are tied more to activities associated with social roles than to accredited, doctor-tested limitations. Disability was seen as influenced not only by the characteristics of impairments, such as type and severity, but also by how the individual defines a given situation and responds to it, and how others define that situation through their responses and expectations.

Another model which fits in the functional limitation paradigm is the original WHO (1980:27) ICIDH model which had three main components – impairment, disability and handicap. Impairment is defined as "any loss or abnormality of psychological, physiological or anatomical structure or function". There are a couple of points to be noted in relation to this definition; first, the term impairment was interpreted to be more inclusive than disorder and, second, to resolve boundary distinctions that lacked clarity in earlier versions, functional limitations were included with impairments (Altman, 2001). Though functional limitation was not a defined concept but it was inherent in the model. Disability was defined as any restriction or lack (resulting from any impairment) of ability to perform an activity in the manner or within the range considered normal for a human being. Handicap, in the context of health experiences, is a disadvantage for a given individual, resulting from impairment or a disability that limits or prevents the fulfilment of a role that is normal for that individual (WHO, 1980:14). While this definition acknowledges that handicap is a social phenomenon and is moderated by the expectations of the particular group of which the individual is a member, the focus is more on the disadvantage resulting from impairment or disability. This classification became the most commonly used definition of disability among medical practitioners and other professionals, including medical sociologists, thus popularizing the medical model which emphasizes on impairment as cause of disability and handicap. The environment here is seen as neutral and the onus of preventing impairment from turning into a disability or handicap lies with the individual.

Problems with the existing definitions of disability led the WHO to begin the process of developing a new definitional framework for understanding disability, based on a revised ICIDH. A revision process of the 1980 ICIDH, across all three dimensions - Impairment, Disability and Handicap was initiated in 1993. The aim of this work was to provide a more coherent and widely applicable set of classifications, which would be conceptually valid and useful. The new classification system falls within the ecological perspective. The ecological perspective developed in the 1970s as a response to the impairment and functional limitation perspective, however, it gained popularity only in the mid 1990s. Like the latter perspective, the ecological perspective rests on three distinct disability concepts: pathology (or abnormality), impairment and disability. However, it sees disability as resulting from the interaction of impairment, activity limitations and participation restrictions in a specific social or physical environment such as work, home or school.

According to the ICIDH-2 (WHO, 1999:16), in the context of health condition, impairment is defined as "problems in body function or structure as a significant deviation or loss". Limitations in certain functions such as the in ability to carry out a basic function of the body or body part, a concept that was included in 1980 within impairments, is still included in the new version. The new term that was introduced to replace 'disability' is 'activity'. It was defined as the performance of a task or action by an individual (ibid: 18). Specifically, the activity dimension is seen to represent the integrated use of body functions in a purposeful way to perform the individual's life tasks (Altman, 2001). In order to give specific recognition to the environmental influence on handicap, the term was reconceptualised as participation. It was defined as "an individual's involvement in life situations in relation to health conditions, body functions and structures, activities and contextual factors" (WHO, 1999:19). The contextual factors are defined as the features, aspects and attributes of, or objects, structures, human-made organizations, service provision, and agencies in, the physical, social and attitudinal environment in which people live and conduct their lives. The objective of these contextual factors is to present a list of potential objects, structures and organisations, or features, aspects or attributes of things, which might help a person with impairments or activity limitations to increase their level of participation in some domain, or alternatively which might be responsible for decreasing the level of participation.

This ecological perspective on disability was also reflected in the International Classification of Functioning, Disability and Health (ICF), adopted by the World Health Assembly in 2001. The final document was the International Classification of Functioning (ICF), which takes a very strong approach to the social model of disability as against the medical model previously used (DPI, 2005). It however does not mean that the medical aspects are ignored by the ICF; in fact, it is based on an integration of these two opposing models. In order to capture the integration of the various perspectives of functioning, a "bio-psychosocial" approach is used. Thus, ICF attempts to achieve a synthesis, in order to provide a coherent view of different perspectives of health from a biological, individual and social perspective.

ICF belongs to the family of international classifications developed by the World Health Organization (WHO) for application to various aspects of health. The WHO family of international classifications provides a framework to code a wide range of information about health (e.g. diagnosis, functioning and disability, reasons for contact with health services) and uses a standardized common language permitting communication about health and health care across the world in various disciplines and sciences. In WHO's international classifications, health conditions (diseases, disorders, injuries, etc.) are classified primarily in ICD-10, which provides an etiological framework. Functioning and disability associated with health conditions are classified in ICF. ICD-10 and ICF are, therefore, complementary. Functioning is an umbrella term encompassing all body functions, activities and participation; similarly, disability serves as an umbrella term for impairments, activity limitations or participation restrictions. The ICF further recognizes that disability is a universal human experience and not a concern to a minority of humanity, every human being can suffer from a decrement in health and, thereby, experience some disability.

Another model which refers to the larger social context as being very important in the development of disability is the Quebec disability production process model (Figure 1.1) which was developed by a team at University Laval, Quebec, Canada led by social scientist Patrick Fougeyrollas is an archetype of the ecological perspective. The Quebec model contributed greatly to the review and eventual improvement of the ICIDH and rejected the linear cause-and-effect explanation of disability. It presented disability as the interaction of three kinds of factors: personal factors (age, sex and cultural identity), environmental factors (the social context in which the person lives) and life habits (the person's daily activities). The Quebec model shifted the focus from a fixed impairment that is part of a person's organic system to other, more changeable factors that affect that person's participation in society. In the Quebec model, disability depended on the environment in which a person lives and carries out daily activities. If the environment is adapted to the person, the disability can change or even disappear. The Quebec model urges for environmental changes so as to accommodate the entire populace, adopting a pro-active approach for prevention of handicaps and creating equal opportunities for all.

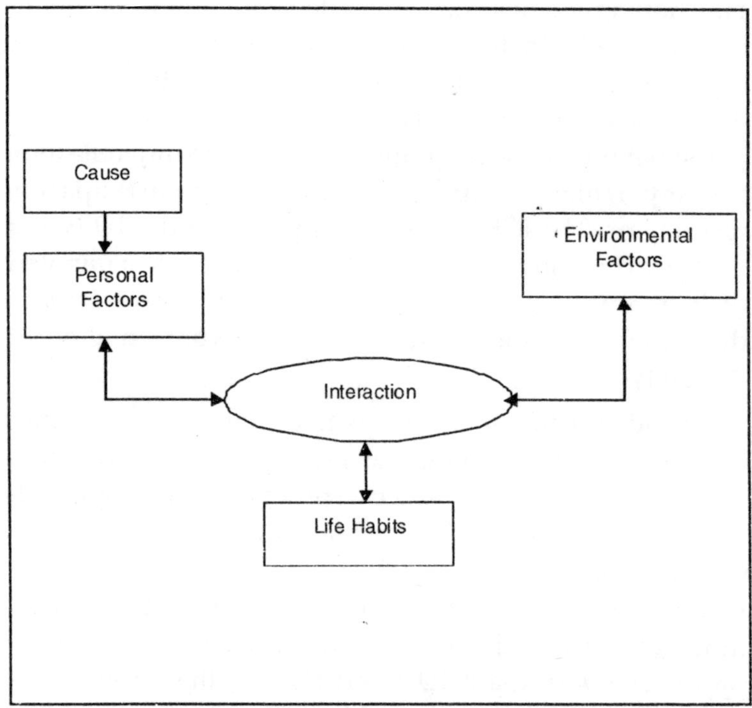

Figure 1.1 : The Quebec Model of Disability

Source: http://www.kuleuven.ac.be/congres/pdf/vettenburg_vandiest.pdf

Another model, which falls under the ecological perspective, is the popular social model of disability and is based on a socio-cultural understanding. It conceives disability as an outcome of social processes or as a constructed or created category. This model focuses on disability as a relationship between people with impairment and a discriminatory society. According to this perspective, disability is considered to be the result of disabling barriers imposed by environmental or policy interventions. The social model suggests a strategy of barrier removal, or education to remove prejudice, with the goal of inclusion (Shakespeare, 1996).

The social model is primarily a consequence of the Disability Rights Movement and has been developed by Disability Studies sociologists. Disability Studies examine the disability as a social, cultural, and political phenomenon. The model does not undermine the medical intervention essential for the present impairment, it advocates for civil rights and self-determination. It challenges the idea that the economic and social statuses and the assigned roles of people with disabilities are inevitable outcomes of their physical, mental or intellectual condition. In contrast to medical or clinical models, social model focuses on how disability is defined and represented in the society. According to this perspective, disability is a construct that finds its meaning in the social and cultural context rather than a characteristic that the person has (Taylor, Shoultz, & Walker, 2003).

The social model rejects the idea of viewing disability as an individual problem caused by impairment. In addition, it denies any causal relationship between having impairment and becoming disabled (Priestly 2003:13). The experience of disability differs for different people in different social, cultural or historical context. For instance, two persons may fit perfectly in one medical criterion of impairment yet their experiences of disability might differ drastically depending on their social or cultural circumstances. Crucially, this view suggests that it is not physical, cognitive or sensory impairments that cause disability, but rather the way the societies fail to accommodate the natural aspects of difference between people (ibid).

Most of what we understand as social model has emanated from the definitions of the disability put forward by the UPIAS. UPIAS (1976:3) contended that "Disability is something *imposed on top* of our impairments by the way we are *unnecessarily isolated and excluded* from full participation in society. Disabled people are, therefore, an *oppressed group* in society" [emphasis added]. A speculation on this definition reveals that disability as a category has been forced upon people with impairments by the society, which has led to their obligatory isolation and exclusion, thus oppressing the disabled people.

From the point of view of disabled people who were setting out to achieve full social integration from the extremity of social deprivation in segregated residential institutions, they encountered seven elements in the following logical order which they dubbed as 'seven needs' (Davis, 1990) – information, counselling, housing, technical aids, personal assistance, transport and access.

Davis (1990) contended that though these needs were natural for anyone to have, these were invariably turned into 'special needs' by the so called 'normal' populace in order to perpetuate the able-bodied culture. "These 'special' needs were thus indicators of just how deeply discriminatory able-bodied practices had penetrated the social structure. The presentation and communication of information favoured sighted and hearing people; the built environment of streets, buildings and houses were designed without regard for the needs of people with mobility impairments; public transport systems were designed and organised to suit the able-bodied; and if the range of implements, tools and devices produced for everyday use, also served disabled people's needs – it was certainly more by accident than design" (ibid: 7-8).

This observation indicated that the artificially created needs by the able-bodied populace leads to discrimination and oppression. The unfulfilled basic needs prevent their full participation and denies them equal status in the society. Hence disability, according to the social model, is all the things that impose restrictions on disabled people; ranging from individual prejudice to institutional discrimination, from inaccessible buildings to unusable transport systems, from segregated education to excluding work arrangements, and so on. Further, the consequences of this failure do not simply and randomly fall on individuals but systematically upon disabled people as a group who experience this failure as discrimination institutionalized throughout society (Oliver, 1996:33 cited in Priestly, 2003).

The human rights model is a distinct subgroup of the social model. It understands disability as a social construct. The human rights model positions disability as an important dimension of human culture, and it affirms that all human beings irrespective of their disabilities have certain rights which are inalienable. By emphasising that the disabled are equally entitled to rights as others, this model builds upon the spirit of the Universal Declaration of Human Rights, 1948, according to which, 'all human beings are born free and equal in rights and dignity' (Rioux, 2005). The human rights model finds its basis in the disability rights movements, which are predicated on the notion that it is the structural and attitudinal barriers in capitalist society that are the fundamental cause for the discrimination and oppression faced by disabled people. In this framework, disabled people are handicapped by the systemic lack of wheelchair access to public services, the failure of educational institutions and employers to make materials available in alternative formats for blind and visually impaired people, and the intricate bureaucracy that disabled people must navigate in order to get essential services such as income support and medical services. Hence, attention needs to be redirected from the medical impairment or medical model of disablement to the social-political issues that underpin disability oppression. In other words, the first step in the liberation of disabled people is a fundamental paradigm shift (Malhotra, 2000).

Four core values of human rights law are of particular importance in the context of disability (UN, 2003):

- the dignity of each individual, who is deemed to be of inestimable value because of his/her inherent self-worth, and not because s/he is economically or otherwise "useful";
- the concept of autonomy or self-determination, which is based on the presumption of a capacity for self-directed action and behaviour, and requires that the person be placed at the centre of all decisions affecting him/her;
- the inherent equality of all regardless of difference; and
- the ethic of solidarity, which requires society to sustain the freedom of the person with appropriate social supports.

The Convention on the Rights of Persons with disabilities was promulgated in 2006 by the United Nations. The Convention (UN, 2006: Article 1) defines persons with disabilities as those who have long-term physical, mental, intellectual or sensory impairments which in interaction with various barriers may hinder their full and effective participation in society on an equal basis with others. The rights-based approach to disability essentially signifies viewing persons with disabilities as subjects of law. Its final aim is to empower disabled persons, and to ensure their active participation in political, economic, social, and cultural life in a way that is respectful and accommodating of their difference. This approach is normatively based on international human rights standards and operationally directed to enhancing the promotion and protection of the human rights of persons with disabilities. Strengthening the protection of human rights is also a way to prevent disability.

The models have given an adequate understanding of the historical transition of the definitions, perspective and thought systems about disability. These models are reflected in the changing policies and programmes of the statutory and non-statutory bodies entrusted with the responsibility of providing the required services for the disabled populace. It would be imperative to look at the relevance and impact of these models on public opinion and policy.

Contextualizing Models to India

It is evident that historical and cultural context determines to a great degree how the criteria for normality, and the ideal or acceptable person, are defined. (Aristotle, 1260 cited in Vehmas). The rehabilitation practices of a society could be comprehended by taking a deeper look at the cultural nuances and responses to disability. Societies develop their characteristic patterns of responding to disability, depending on the way disability is understood and their resources then identified. Historical events, sacred texts, social institutions, and so on, all contribute in the social construction of disablement. Therefore, it may be imperative to take a closer look at the cultural and social constructs of disability in India so as to examine the traditional and current approaches to disability rehabilitation and their relevance in the changing global scenario. However, India being such a vast country, it is difficult to think in terms of a unified-single culture that is prevalent everywhere. Indian society has always remained pluralistic with multiple traditions.

Indians, in general, have an ambivalent attitude towards people with disability. In dealing with someone with a disability, people are caught in an avoid-help kind of a conflicting situation and feel anxious. All religions believe in the concept of divine retribution; inflicting disability is a way of awarding punishment to the sinner of previous births by God. The other notion is that pain in the form of disability is inflicted on people whose resilience God wishes to test. Another prevalent belief is that charity and compassion towards the less fortunate (disabled) by the fortunate people would earn them advantage. *Manu Smriti*, the ancient charter of social conduct impelled people to spare a part of their material resources for their hapless fellow-beings; to support their daily living (Prabhu 1963). *Dharmashastra* called upon all householders to look after the weak and disabled, and those who did do so, were ensured a place in heaven (Kuppuswamy, 1977).

In Indian and other Asian societies, the concept of *karma* governs basic assumptions about disability, where disability is seen as the result of sins committed in previous births (Ghai, 2001, Karna, 2001 cited in Ghosh, 2005). The theory of *karma* is propounded to explain all kinds of suffering. This theory implies that if one has committed misdeeds in previous births, one has to inevitably bear the consequences. Disability is held to be a punishment for the sins of previous births and one is called upon to accept it as divine retribution. This notion of a just world is firmly ingrained in the minds of the people and is frequently invoked to explain whatever happens in one's life (Paranjpe, 1986). This thought system which has descended from our religious texts has given rise to charity driven interventions, which are intended to be beneficial. There is little understanding that it is actually compromising their beneficiaries' rights. Since entitlement to rights is often substituted by relief measures, over which the groups declared invalid have little control or power to bargain, the charity model creates an army of powerless individuals dependent on either State sponsored charities or arrangements maintained by benevolent individuals outside mainstream development and mechanisms of social support. Special schools, sheltered workshops and protection homes for persons with disabilities were established throughout the country by religious and other philanthropic agencies.

The shift in policy and legislation in India has seen a major change after ratification of the various international conventions, which has been reflected in its legislations and policies. The Government of India has enacted three legislations for persons with disabilities, namely:

(i) Persons with Disability (Equal Opportunities, Protection of Rights and Full Participation) Act, 1995, which provides for education, employment, creation of barrier free environment, social security, etc. The promulgation of the Persons with Disabilities (Equal Opportunities, Protection of Rights and Full Participation) Act, 1995 was to give effect to the Proclamation on the Full Participation and Equality of the People with Disabilities in the Asian and Pacific Region adopted by the Economic and Social Commission for Asia and Pacific held at Beijing in 1992. Even though the new legislation is more than a decade old, there have not been any significant development towards implementation of the Act.

(ii) National Trust for Welfare of Persons with Autism, Cerebral Palsy, Mental Retardation and Multiple Disability Act, 1999 has provisions for legal guardianship of the four categories and creation of enabling environment for as much independent living as possible.

(iii) Rehabilitation Council of India Act, 1992 deals with the development of manpower for providing rehabilitation services.

These legislations if analysed through the model perspectives on disability reflect that though the constructs of disability are largely medical, it takes on a rights based approach. The Act guarantees full equality, independence and accessibility to all people with disabilities to the services and facilities needed in day-to-day living.

The National Policy for Persons with Disability, 2006, attempts to clarify the framework under which the state, civil society and private sector must operate in order to ensure a dignified life for persons with disability and support for their caregivers. It includes extending rehabilitation services to rural areas, increasing trained personnel to meet needs, emphasizing education and training, increasing employment opportunities, focusing on gender equality, improving access to public services, encouraging state governments to develop a comprehensive social security policy, ensuring equal opportunities in sports, recreation and cultural activities, increasing the role of civil society organisations as service-providers to persons with disability and their families.

The ratification of international covenants calls for commitment and action at three levels – legislative, financial and ideological. Whenever an act or policy is enacted following ratification of a convention, its implementation depends on the financial and ideological commitment the nation's government shows towards change. The Indian government has developed four national level institutes for specific disabilities. However, the prime objective of these institutes is rehabilitation. Though the government relies heavily on the voluntary sector for provision of basic facilities, it has allocated only 30 per cent of the planned expenditure on the voluntary sector and the rest is reserved for the national institutes and factories it has set for aids and appliances (Alur, 2002) for meeting their rehabilitation objectives, which are mostly health and welfare oriented.

The international statutes uphold the social model of disability and reject the charitable model or construction of disability as a problem located in the disabled individual who possesses medical needs. A high proportion of social welfare policies and traditional charities subscribe to the medical point of view, in which disabled people are rendered dependent passive recipients of charity (Chib, 2002). Though in legislations, there is a mention of inclusive practices and ensuring rights and independence to the people with disabilities, the practice shows coexistence of these social, medical and charitable perspectives. The international policies aim towards equity and equal opportunities of disabled people in all spheres, their translation at national level has been reduced to formulating policies in keeping with the ratified covenants which lack effective implementation.

Conclusion

The chapter has endeavoured to discuss the different paradigms on disability constructs. It looked at the existing models within the three key paradigms - the impairment perspective, the functional perspective and the ecological perspective. It attempted to trace how these models evolved through the activism and struggle of the disabled population. It also tried to see the relevance of these models in designing services and programmes for the disabled in Indian context.

There is little doubt that the changing perspectives on disability and the resultant models have tremendously affected the service provision and policy formulation for the disabled. The disabled population worldwide has upheld and promoted the social construct of disability, which has gradually replaced the older medically rigid definitions of disability. Oliver (1996a) noted in his article that the social model of disability has been the foundation upon which disabled people have chosen to organize themselves collectively. This has resulted in unparalleled success in changing the discourses around disability, in promoting disability as a civil rights issue and in developing schemes to give disabled people autonomy and control in their own lives. This is surely reflected in the international conventions and has thus percolated to the policies and programmes of the member states.

The UN Standard Rules on the Equalization of Opportunities for Persons with Disabilities (1993) is a good reflection of the shifting perspective of disability at the international platform. The rules emphasize that disability is a socially created problem and not an attribute of an individual. Disablement results from a dynamic interaction between health conditions and other personal factors (such as age, sex, personality or level of education) on the one hand, and social and physical environmental factor on the other hand.

Rule 14 of the document recommends the following guidelines for ensuring that disability aspects are included in all relevant policy-making and national planning :

- States should initiate and plan adequate policies for persons with disabilities at the national level, and stimulate and support action at regional and local levels.
- States should involve organizations of persons with disabilities in all decision-making relating to plans and programmes concerning persons with disabilities or affecting their economic and social status.
- The needs and concerns of persons with disabilities should be incorporated into general development plans and not be treated separately.
- The ultimate responsibility of States for the situation of persons with disabilities does not relieve others of their responsibility. Anyone in charge of services, activities or the provision of information in society should be encouraged to accept responsibility for

making such programmes available to persons with disabilities.

- States should facilitate the development by local communities of programmes and measures for persons with disabilities. One way of doing this could be to develop manuals or check-lists and provide training programmes for local staff.

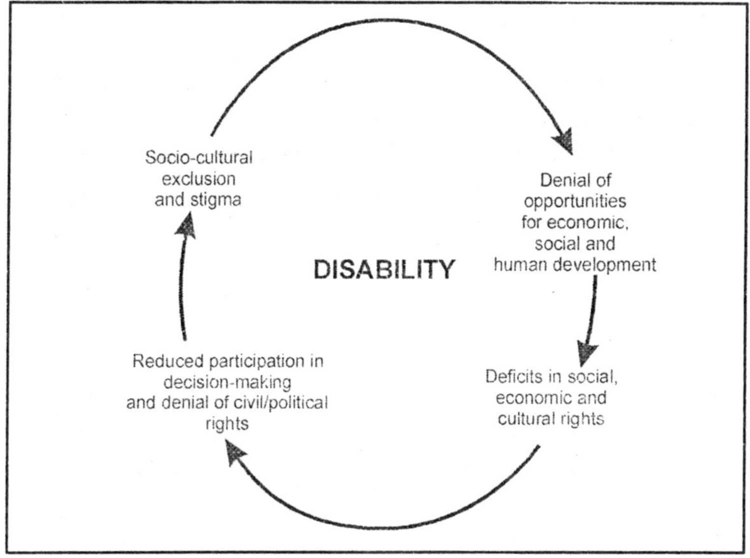

Figure 1.2: Probable Consequences of Disability.

Source: Adapted from DFID (2000:4)

These policies and programmes must aim to mitigate the adverse outcomes of disability (see Figure 1.2), which may form a vicious cycle. A disability under an adverse environment may lead to denial of basic opportunities which may cause deficits in social, economic and cultural rights like food and clean water, adequate housing and shelter, health, education, right to work, linguistic rights, access to places of entertainment, sports and culture, access to Media and Information Communication Technologies (ICTs). These deprivations and deficits reduce their fair chances of participation in the 'normal' activities, ultimately leading to their marginalisation and social exclusion. It is, therefore, important to understand the perspective and demands of the disabled population in order to design programmes and policies for them. It means they require adequate participation in decision-making process as suggested by the international covenants.

It was interesting to note that though the ecological perspective, which aims towards enhancing abilities and restructuring the society, has widely featured by the recent international conventions and subsequent legislations and policies in the member states, its understanding and acceptability by the non-disabled population is not widespread. Most often than not, people align with the impairment perspective that refers to the fact that some people are different from others in ways that are not desirable. They are considered disabled and thus in need of medical care, special education, vocational rehabilitation and a host of services to cure them, if possible, or to help them adjust to their afflictions, if recovery is not possible. Their impairments are diagnosed and evaluated, plans (for treatment, education or rehabilitation) are prescribed, and professionally directed courses of action are followed to assist these individuals in reaching some predetermined goals. From this perspective, one recognizes that disability may be a highly personal experience and that individual functional improvements are possible and even advantageous to the person involved. Efforts are directed at overcoming unfortunate odds through rehabilitation, education and technology. Recognition is given to the systemic and ecological barriers that must be faced and some approaches to lessening these include special transportation, assistive technology development, public relations campaigns etc. to name a few.

While this common sense notion of disability still pervades our country and its so called welfare programmes, attaining social equity is a far fledged aspiration. The reality is that the ideas, conceptualizations and related actions embellish the legislations and policies and the awareness regarding disability issues, the rights of the disabled and their equivalent social status is very low amongst the 'normal' populace. A necessitated action in this regard is to raise responsiveness of the people on these issues and empower the differentially able population to fight for their rights as equal human beings.

References

Altman, Barbara M. (2001). Disability Definitions, Models, Classification Schemes and Applications. In Gary L. Albrecht, Katherine D. Seelman and Michael Bury (Eds.), *Handbook of Disability Studies*. Thousand Oaks (Cal.): Sage Publications.

Alur, M. (2002). Special Needs Policy in India. In Seamus Hegarty and Mithu Alur (Eds.), *Education and Children with Special Needs - From Segregation to Inclusion*. New Delhi: Sage Publications Inc.

Brisenden, Simon (1986). Independent Living and the Medical Model of Disability. In Tom Shakespeare (Ed.), *The Disability Reader: Social Science Perspectives*. London: Cassell (1998).

Chib, Malini (2002). In Seamus Hegarty and Mithu Alur (Eds.), *Education and Children with Special Needs - From Segregation to Inclusion*. New Delhi: Sage Publications Inc.

Davis, Ken (1990). *A Social Barriers Model of Disability: Theory into Practice*. The Emergence of the "Seven Needs" Paper prepared for the Derbyshire Coalition of Disabled People: February, 1990. *Source*: http://www.leeds.ac.uk/disability-studies/archiveuk/DavisK/davis-social%20barriers.pdf (Retrieved on 3rd January 2007)

DFID (2000). *Disability, Poverty and development. Source*: http://www.dfid.gov.uk/pubs/files/disabilitypovertydevelopment.pdf Retrieved on 6th October 2006.

Disabled People International (2005). http://v1.dpi.org/lang-en/resources/details.php?page=74 (Date of Retrieval : 17th October 2006)

Driedgar, Diane (1989). *The Last Civil Rights Movement: Disabled Peoples' International*. London: Hurst and Company.

Finkelstein, V. (1991). Disability and Administrative Challenge. In Michael Oliver (Ed.), *Social Work: Disabled People and Disabling Environments*. London: Jessica Kingsley Publishers Ltd.

Ghosh, Nandini (2005). *The Concept of Disability*. Unpublished Pre Doctoral Paper. Mumbai: Tata Institute of Social Sciences.

Groschl, Stefan (2005). Persons with Disabilities: A Source of Nontraditional Labor for Canada's Hotel Industry. *Cornell Hotel and Restaurant Administration Quarterly*, Volume 46, Number 2 258-274. New York: Cornell University

Kuppuswamy, B. (1977) *Dharma and Society*. New Delhi: Macmillan.

Malhotra, Ravi (2000). The Politics of Disability Rights Movement. *New Politics*, 8(3) 12-17.

Miller, E.J. and G.V. Gwynne (1972). *A Life Apart*. London: Tavistock Publications.

Nagi, Saad Z. (1965). "Some conceptual issues in Disability and Rehabilitation". In M. Sussman (ed.). *Sociology and Rehabilitation*. Washington, DC: American Sociological Association.

Oliver, Mike (1983). Social Work with Disabled People. Basingstoke: Macmillans.

Oliver, Mike (1990 a). *The Individual and Social Models of Disability*. Paper presented at Joint Workshop of the Living Options Group and the Research Unit of the Royal College of Physicians on People with Established Locomotor Disabilities in Hospitals Monday 23 July 1990. http://www.leeds.ac.uk/disabilitystudies/archiveuk/Oliver/in%20soc%20dis.pdf (Date of Retrieval: 25th September 2006).

Oliver, Mike (1990 b). *The Politics of Disablement*. Basingstoke: Macmillans.

Oliver, Mike (1996). Defining Impairment and Disability: Issues at Stake. In Colin Barnes and Geof Mercer (Eds.), *Exploring the Divide*. Leeds: The Disability Press, pp.29-54.

Oliver, Michael J. 1999. "Capitalism, disability and ideology: A materialist critique of the Normalization principle." First published in Flynn, Robert J. and Raymond A. Lemay, *A Quarter-Century of Normalization and Social Role Valorization: Evolution and Impact, 1999*. Internet publication URL: http://www.independentliving.org/docs3/oliver99.pdf

Paranjpe A.C. (1986). *Theoretical Psychology : Meeting of East and West*. New York: Plenum Press.

Prabhu, P.N., (1963). *Hindu Social Organizations*. Bombay: Popular Prakashan.

Priestly, Mark (2003). *Disability: A Life Course Approach*. Cambridge: Polity Press.

Rioux, Marcia (2005). *Approaches to Disability. In National Human Rights Commission Disability Manual*. New Delhi: NHRC.

Schumpeter, J.A. (1975). *History of Economic Analysis*. New York: Oxford University Press.

Shakespeare, T. (1996). *Disability, identity and difference.* Leeds, UK: The Disability Press, 94-113. Retrieved October 7, 2006, from http://www.leeds.ac.uk/disability-studies/archiveuk/Shakespeare/Chap6.pdf

Taylor, S., Shoultz, B., & Walker, P. (2003). *Disability Studies: Information and Resources.* Retrieved May 6, 2005, from http://thechp.syr.edu/Disability_Studies_2003_current.html

United Nations (1993).*The Standard Rules on the Equalization of Opportunities for Persons with Disabilities.* New York: Author.

United Nations (2003) Retrieved from http://www.unhchr.ch/disability/intro.htm#human on 9th January 2007

United Nations (2006). Convention on the Rights of Persons with Disabilities. Retrieved on 3rd January 2007 from http://www.un.org/esa/socdev/enable/rights/convtexte.htm

UPIAS (1976). *Fundamental Principles of Disability. London*: Union of the Physically Impaired Against Segregation

Vehmas, Simo (2004) *Ethical Analysis of the Concept of Disability.* Mental Retardation, Vol. 42, No. 3, pp. 209-222.

World Health Organisation (1980). *International Classification of Impairments, Disabilities, and Handicaps: A Manual of Classification Relating to the Consequences of Disease.* Geneva: Author.

World Health Organisation (1999). ICIDH-2: International Classification of Functioning and Disability. Beta-2 draft, full version. Geneva: Author.

2

CHILDREN WITH SPECIAL NEEDS
Family Responses

Introduction

Hartman and Laird (1983:4) have noted, "Human beings can be understood and helped only in the context of the intimate and powerful human systems of which they are a part," an important component of which is the family. Most imperative functions of the family are to rear and educate children so that they are prepared to be independent, self-sufficient and productive in the society. A child's behaviour and thought reflects his parenting and family environment. Family assumes a greater importance when the child has some special needs to which it needs to cater.

Birth of a child is a major event for a family as its arrival is anxiously awaited. However, the birth of the child with special needs in a family is looked upon as a setback. The emotions associated with the birth of such a child could be shock, depression, guilt, anger, sadness, and anxiety. It turns out to be a very stressful for the members of the family to cater to the varied needs of the child. The problem increases manifold when the family is unable to accept the different child. All families handle their situation differently and may stay in certain stages longer than the others. It is indeed significant for the family to realise that the child with disability needs the parents and family as much as the non-disabled child.

The societal attitudes towards marriage and childbirth significantly influence the adaptation of family to birth of an exceptional child. Society has always desired blissful union of a couple to produce physically and mentally healthy children (Greer, 1975). Such an expectation from the society causes families to suffer more at the advent of birth of a child with exceptionalities. It reacts in different ways to suppress their feelings. Bauer and Shea (1987) presented an integrated perspective on family, adaptation to the birth or diagnosis of a child with exceptionality. According to them, adjustment becomes a developmental process that is attempt to meet both the parents' and child's needs. "Family adaptation is seen as occurring within several nested personal, familial, social and cultural contexts" (Shea and Bauer, 1991: 23).

It was during the 1960s when there was a research emphasis on parents having a child with special needs. There were many approaches, which helped in finding answers to a couple of crucial questions: the nature of parental reaction to having a child with special needs and the source of this reaction (Ferguson, 2001). Many researchers to look for common descriptions for parents having a child with special needs followed the psychodynamic approach that has its roots in Freudianism. Hostility, denial, guilt, grief, defence mechanism of all types, and a positive goal of acceptance were all prominent terms in the traditional profile of parental reactions. Most of the research conducted in this area used attitudinal categories to portray neurotic paths the families followed (Pinkerton, 1972). In the 1960s and 1970s, there was a shift in ideology and preference for behavioural approaches over the previously prevalent psychoanalytic tradition was noticed. The behavioural emphasis in family research helped to provide practical aids to the parents who show dysfunctional tendencies to allow them to interact effectively with their children (Ferguson, 2001). Another prevalent approach around the same time was the psychosocial approach emphasizing the interplay of parental emotions with the environmental circumstances in which the family found itself (ibid). One of the first examples of this approach is Olshansky's (1962) classic description of "chronic sorrow" (Wikler, Wasow, and Hatfield, 1981). This approach identifies chronic sorrow as a normal, understandable reaction to an unexpected and unwarranted situation (Ferguson 2001). Wolfensberger (1983) described a pattern of psychosocial orientation to parental reactions as "novelty shock." The emphasis of a novelty shock interpretation is that an unanticipated event occurs, producing initial reactions of bewilderment, confusion and dismay. Instead of the disability itself, the crucial factor is now seen as the social communication of information and interpretive stances taken by professionals and family members (Ferguson, 2001). The least common approach of the four options was the Interactionist Approach. Indeed, this interpretational orientation arose more from parent narratives themselves than from professional inquiry (Featherstone, 1980; Ferguson & Heifetz, 1983; Massie & Massie, 1975).

There were four major theoretical perspectives which have guided research on families of children with special needs: (a) stage theory models which explain the patterns of adjustment which parents demonstrate while coping with the birth or diagnosis of the child with special needs(see Parks, 1977; Blacher, 1984), (b) stress and coping models which describe the stress/crisis that precipitates due to the birth or special needs throughout the developmental span of the child (see Duis, Summers, and Summers, 1997), (c) family system models wherein several aspects of the family system are studied in relation to parenting the child with disability (see Mink, Nihira and Meyers, 1983; Mink, Meyers and Nihira 1984), and (d) social ecology models where the family system is studied with respect to the environment (see Gallimore, Coots, Weisner, Garnier and Guthrie, 1996) (Hauser-Cram and Howell, 2003:522-23).

The chapter is an elucidation of various theories which have guided the researches on psychosocial responses of families having children with special needs. The subsequent sections would review and contextualize various Family Models to the families of the children with special needs. The final segment of the chapter would endeavour to compare and critique the models and would end with the reflection of the learning from these on the intervention arena.

The Stage Theory Models

Having an infant with disability is often experienced by parents as the death of the expected normal, healthy child. It has been suggested that parents of a child with a disability have to go through the grieving process (denial, bargaining, anger, depression, and acceptance) in order to accept their child's handicapping condition (Seligman & Darling, 1989: 86). In the past these stages of grieving (Kubler-Ross, 1969) although not viewed as linear, have generally been presented as relevant to the grieving process of parents of a child with a disability as they move from one stage to the next and finally, towards acceptance of their child's condition.

In this adaptation, acceptance has been considered to be reached when the parent presents a realistic view of their child's disability both in type and degree. Unresolved grief has in turn been interpreted as a lack of acceptance of the child's disability. Therefore, there is a need to explicate the stage theory model and also look at the research work, which have impacted this area.

The Stage Theory of grieving was developed by Kubler-Ross in relation to death and dying. The different stages of grieving has been described as:

1. **Denial and Isolation :** When the news is broken to the parents, they go through an initial denial phase. "No, not me, it cannot be true" (Kubler-Ross, 1969:34). Denial or at least partial denial is used by most parents not only during the first stages of the diagnosis but also later on from time to time. "Denial functions as a buffer after an unexpected shocking news, allows the patient to collect himself and with time, mobilize other, less radical defences" (ibid, p. 35). In context of parents having a child with special needs "patient" could be read as "parent". Denial is usually a temporary defense and is sooner/later replaced by partial acceptance.
2. **Anger:** "When the first stage of denial cannot be maintained any longer, it is replaced by feelings of anger, rage, envy and resentment. The next line of enquiry is, "Why me?" (ibid, p. 44). In comparison to the earlier stage of denial, this stage is difficult to cope with as anger may find other outlets like displacement or projection onto the environment at times almost at random.
3. **Bargaining:** The second stage of anger is also temporary and paves way to bargaining. "the bargaining is really an attempt to postpone; it has to include a prize offered 'for good behaviour', it also sets a self-imposed 'deadline', and it includes a promise that the patient will not ask for more, if this postponement is granted" (p. 73). Most bargains are made with God and kept a closely guarded secret.

4. **Depression:** When the parents could no longer deny their child's illness, when the medical procedures take their toll, when the child displays the symptoms, their denial or anger is replaced by sense of great loss. They become depressed.
5. **Acceptance:** When the parents have had enough time and have been given help in working through the previously described stages, they are neither depressed nor angry about their fate (p. 99). Acceptance should not be, however, mistaken for a happy stage. It is almost void of feelings. It is as if the pain has gone and the struggle is over.

Contextualizing parental reactions to the birth of the child with special needs has been attempted by many researchers. Turnbull and Blacher-Dixon (1980) had identified three stages of adjustment that parents of children with special need experience. The initial stage is that of shock and denial, in which parents refuse to acknowledge the reality or at least the extent of their child's delay in an effort to believe that a cure or magical intervention could prevent any lifelong problem. The second stage is characterized by intellectual awareness of the problem but some reactions like anger, disappointment, grief or guilt may occur. The third stage is that of emotional adjustment which represents constructive adaptation to child's handicap and realistic expectation of his/her progress (cited in Blacher, 1984).

Farber (1975) had hypothesized six phases of successive adaptation through which the family of the child with special needs may progress. The first is the labelling phase, in which the basis for the existing role arrangements are removed and there is a realization that major assumptions underlying family relationships have to be renegotiated. When the child fails to develop as per the normal standards the parents may use garb of less offensive labels and dread the most stigmatizing ones. For instance, a child with down syndrome may be thought of by the parents as having a slight speech impediment correctable by speech therapy. The second phase, normalization where the family tries to handle the deviant child within the existing norms.

The family may use some of these strategies to accomplish this: (1) the perceptions of the family members regarding the existence of the problem may be suppressed, (2) some members may convince others to change their perceptions, or (3) some may pretend that there is no problem. In the third phase, mobilization, the family could no longer manage with the existing arrangements and therefore, it makes adaptations affecting all family members. In the revisionist fourth phase, the family discovers that minor revisions in the family roles are not sufficient and what is required most is the change in basic role structure of the family. The fifth phase, polarization occurs as interaction between the family members decreases. They coexist with little sharing and often without fulfilling negotiated roles. The final phase is termed as elimination, where the child is frequently blamed for the tension in the family and institutionalization may be the next recourse (cited in Wright *et al.* 1984). It was acknowledged by Farber that some families may skip certain phases of the process, or complex adaptations may precede simple ones.

The literature on hypothesized stages of adjustment yields an unclear picture as to (1) whether the stages can, in fact, be empirically validated, (2) whether they are experienced in a particular order, (3) the amount of time it takes to move through each stage emotionally, and (4) whether ultimate parental acceptance or emotional adjustment is related to the degree of the child's handicap (Blacher, 1984:28). There has been a study by Eden in 1983, which has provided empirical support for the existence of these stages. He proposed five stages, (1) shock, confusion, (2) refusal, denial, (3) guilt, anger, (4) despair, depression, and (5) adjustment, recovery, acceptance. Where the several stages were empirically validated, the final stage of acceptance was found not to be single isolated outcome. It emerged from the analysis that acceptance could be attained in levels within each factor or stage as it was found to be a fluid concept as opposed to what was originally proposed in literature.

However, the stage theory models have suitably addressed the micro level issues concerning parental reaction to the birth/diagnosis of their child with special needs and their consequent adaptation which occurs in phases. Though many studies have drawn considerably from these models, the newer advances in research have broadened their focus to include the environmental effects. The chapter would now look at the other theoretical models which have impacted research in the last three decades.

The Family Stress Models

Families are viewed as social system which constantly tries to maintain a steady state. Families are the products of both subsystems (e.g. individual members, dyads) and suprasystems (e.g. community, culture, nation). Families do not live in isolation; they are part of the larger social context. According to the social systems theory the family is embedded in an external environment which is referred to as the ecosystem. The ecosystem consists of historical, cultural, genetic and developmental influences (Boss 1988). Hence, the family responds to a stressor event depending on its cultural identification, economic conditions of society, its genetic stamina and resistance and its stage in the family life cycle (McKenry and Price, 2000). A closer look at the some of the family stress models would help in explicating the causal factors of stress and coping behaviours.

ABC-X Model

The model was propounded by Hill in 1949. Though the model has been expanded (McCubbin and Patterson, 1980; Patterson, 1988), the basis retains its original nature.

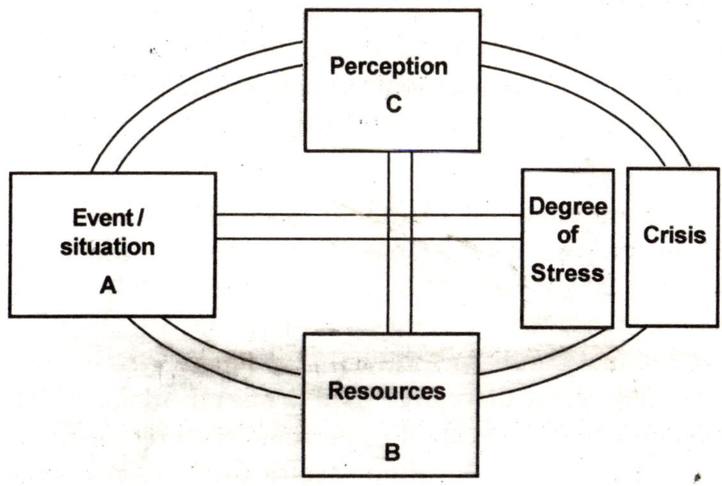

Figure 2.1 : ABC-X Model of Family Crisis
Source: Hill (1958).

The family stress described in Figure 2.1 could be stated as A (the provoking stressor event) interacting with B (family resources and strengths, interacting with C (the definition or meaning attached to the event by family), produces X (stress or crisis). The figure clearly indicates that stress is not an outcome of the stressor event purely; it is influenced by several other factors, which act as moderators or buffers.

Stressor Events (A)

A stressor event is an occurrence that provokes a variable amount of change in the family system. The degree of stress generated depends upon the magnitude of the stress as well as the moderating factors. Family stress researchers often use a dichotomous classification; normal or predictable events *versus* non-normative or unpredictable or situational events. Normal events are part and parcel of our daily lives and represent transitions inherent in family life cycle, such as the birth and death of a family member. Normative stressor events by definition are of shorter duration (Carter and McGoldrick, 1989). Non-normative events are the product of some unique situation that could not have been predicted (Boss, 1988).

Resources (B)

The family resources buffer or moderate the impact of the stressor event on the family's level of stress (McKenry and Price 2000). McCubbin and Patterson (1985) define resources as traits, characteristics or abilities of (a) individual family members, (b) the family system, and (c) the community that can be used to meet the demands of a stressor event. Individual or personal resources include financial security, education, health that encompasses physical, mental and spiritual well-being, and psychological resources. Family system resources are the internal attributes of the family that guard against negative effects of stress, crisis or both. Family cohesion (bonds of unity) and adaptability (ability to change) (Olson, Russell and Sprenkle, 1979, 1983) have received quit a lot of research attention. Community resources refer to those capabilities of people or institutions outside the family on which the family can draw for dealing with stress. Social support is one of the most important community resources, though it could be provided by family members as well (McKenry and Price, 2000). Social support offers information at an interpersonal level that provides (a) emotional support, (b) esteem support, and (c) network support (Cobb, 1976). The concept of community resources has been broadened to include resources of cultural groups; for example, ethnic minority families are thought to be characterized by more elaborate and efficient patterns of social support (Hill, 1999; McCubbin, Futrell, Thompson, and Thompson, 1998).

Definition of the Event/Perceptions (C)

The impact of the stressor event on the family's level of stress is also moderated by the definition or meaning the family gives to the event. The subjective definition could vary from that the circumstances are a challenge posed to the family or an opportunity for growth to some negative attitudes like things are hopeless, too difficult or manageable (McCubbin and Patterson, 1985). If families are able to redefine the situation in order to lessen the emotional burden and be more responsive to the stressor, they are better able to cope and adapt.

Stress and Crisis

According to the social systems theory, stress represents a change in the family's steady state. The degree of stress experienced by the family depends on the family resources to meet the demands of the change associated with the stressor event (McCenry and Price 2000). It is important to distinguish between the sometimes synonymously used terms stress and crisis. Boss (1988) attempted to make a clear distinction between the two when she defined crisis as a disturbance, which is so overwhelming, pressure that is so severe or change that is so acute that the family system is blocked, immobilized and incapacitated. Family stress is merely a state of changed or disturbed equilibrium.

The major emphasis in family stress research during the 1970s and 1980s shifted from crisis to coping. Researchers started concentrating more on why families succeed rather than why families fail (McCubbin, Joy *et al.* 1980; McCubbin and Boss, 1980).

During the 1970s, a new concept called coping was introduced into the family stress literature (Boss, McCubbin and Lester, 1979; McCubbin, 1979; McCubbin, Dahl, Lester, Benson and Robertson, 1976). This added a new dimension to the existing Hill's ABC-X model. An adaptation of Hill's model to accommodate coping is illustrated in Figure 2.2.

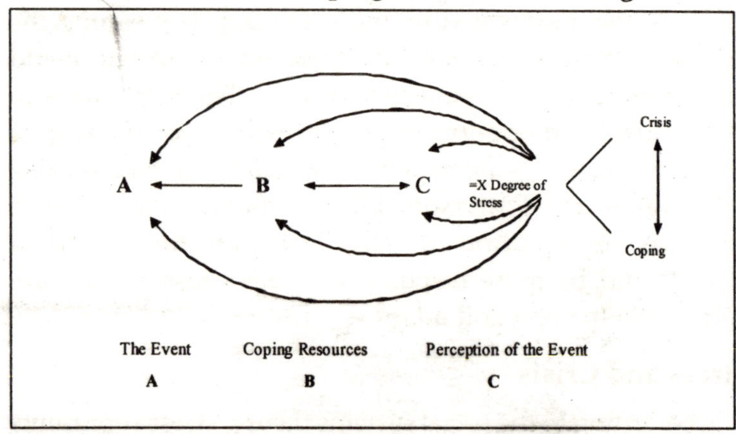

Figure 2.2: Hill's ABC-X Model revised to show the degree of stress and alternative outcomes of crisis and coping

Source: Boss (1987: 702).

McCubbin and Patterson (1982) had expanded Hill's ABC-X model by adding postcrisis/poststress factors in order to explain how families achieve a satisfactory adaptation to stress or crisis. Their model consists of the ABC-X model followed by their Double ABC-X configuration. (See Figure 2.3).

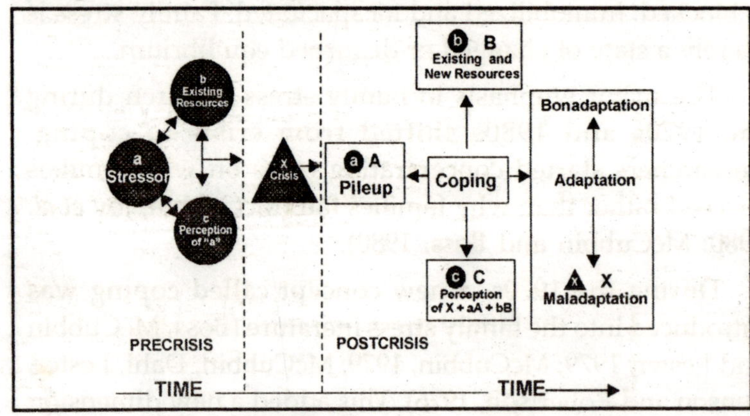

Figure 2.3 : Double ABC-X Model

Source: McCubbin and Patterson (1982).

This version of the model has added other variables in an attempt to describe the process of adaptation over time. In the Double ABCX model, for example, there is also a "pile-up" of other stressors (aA), the family's new and existing resources (bB), and a slightly modified meaning of the stressor (cC) which are used to predict family adaptation to the crisis (xX).

The "Double A" factor includes three types of stressors. The family must deal with unresolved aspects of the initial stressor event, the changes and events that occur regardless of the initial stressor (e.g., changes in family membership), and the consequences of the family efforts to cope with the hardships of the situation. The family resources, the "Double B" factor are of two types. The first are those resources that are already available to the family and that minimize the impact of the initial stressor. The second are those coping resources (personal, family and social) that are either strengthened or developed in response to the stress or crisis situation. The "Double C" factor refers to the perception of the initial stressor event and the perception of the stress and crisis (McKenry and Price, 2000). Family perception involves an overall assessment of family situation, including the stressor and its hardships, changes made, the family's capability, the compatibility of family changes with member needs and development, and the coordination and synergism of these family changes with all respects of family functioning and system needs (DeMarco *et al.* 2000). The "Double X" factor includes the original family crisis/stress response and subsequent adaptation of the family (McKenry and Price, 2000).

More recent versions of this model are more sophisticated still, including constructs such as problem solving/coping, family typology, and resiliency as family researchers have begun to assess family stress outcomes from a family strengths perspective. The Resiliency Model has as its origin the seminal family stress and coping work of Reuben Hill (1958), the Double ABCX Model of Family Adjustment and Adaptation (McCubbin & Patterson, 1983), and the more recent Typology Model of Family Adjustment and Adaptation (McCubbin & McCubbin, 1989). Focused investigations on what makes the family system resilient in the face of normative transitions as well as catastrophic life events have emerged at a slower pace. Family resiliency has been defined as the property of the family system that enable the family unit to respond constructively to (a) a stressor (in combination with risk factors) and in so doing, maintain its positive function and ensure the well being and development of the family unit and its members (i.e., protective), and (b) disorganization (family crisis brought about by the stressor in combination with risk factors) and in doing so, bounce back amd restore its positive functioning and ensure well-being and development of the family unit and its members (i.e., recovery) (DeMarco, 2000:299).

Within the Family Resiliency framework (McCubbin & McCubbin 1993, 1996) resilience is viewed as involving two distinguishable but related family processes: (1) adjustment, which involves the influence of protective factors in facilitating the family's ability and efforts to maintain its integrity, functioning, and fulfil developmental tasks in the face of risk factors, and (2) adaptation, which involves the function of recovery factors in promoting the family's ability to "bounce back" and adapt in family crisis situations. Consequently, family resilience research has focused on addressing the central and complex issues of determining what protective factors are critical to family adjustment in the face of specific risks or cluster of risk factors as well as what recovery factors are critical to family adaptation in the face of specific family crisis situations.

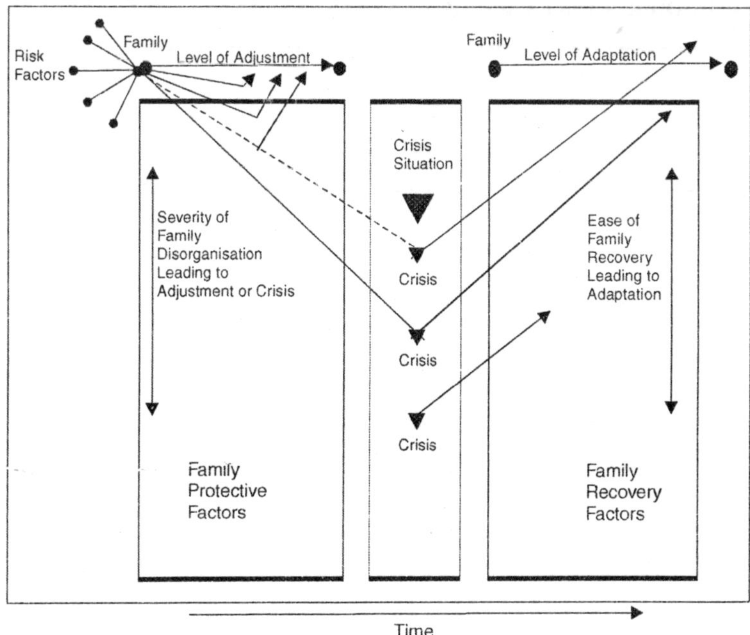

Figure 2.4 : Relationship between risk factors, protective factors, family crises, and recovery factors.

Source: http.//www.cyfernet extension umn. edu/research/resilient.html.

Contextualizing the Family Stress Models

The birth of a child with exceptionality certainly induces stress in a family. Beresford (1994) showed the nature of stress to span over several aspects of family life such as daily care demands, emotional distress (e.g., maternal depression), interpersonal difficulties (e.g., parental discord), financial problems and adverse social consequences (e.g., social isolation). Stress experienced by the families is influenced by child specific variables like age, sex and severity of the problem; socio-demographic variables such as social class, family income and domicile; and family coping resources and strategies like acceptance of the child's diagnosis and perception of stigma associated with the disorder. According to McAndrew (1976), additional stress was also created due to marital conflicts associated with rearing the handicapped child, extra financial burdens to obtain the necessary services, and fatigue and loss of leisure time due to care-taking responsibilities. Singers and Powers (1993) added that not only do child characteristics influence parental stress levels, but negative reactions from others can also serve as a source of stress for the families. Parenting a child with a disability increases stress in the areas of everyday management of disruptive behaviours, heavy caregiving responsibilities, and concerns about the future of the child when the parents are no longer able to care for him or her (cited in Gupta and Singhal 2004). In addition to the stress of the disability itself, financial strain due to medical bills or quality care, lack of control, egos, attitudes, isolation, anger, embarrassment, grief, and protectiveness all merge to bombard the family of a child with a disability (Havens, 2005).

In order to analyze the factors influencing the family's stress response, the ABCX and Double ABCX Models of Family Stress were reviewed. Four factors of the model which are particularly relevant when applied to the experience of the family with a child with special needs are: the specific characteristics of the child's special needs, the family's perception of the stressor, the chronicity of the problem, and the social network of the family.

There have been some interesting and helpful studies of parents of children with Developmental Disabilities conducted using McCubbin & Patterson's (1983) Double ABCX Model or variations on it (e.g., Bristol, 1987; Minnes, 1988; Wikler, 1986). In the original form of this model (Hill, 1949), A represents the stressor or crisis-provoking event (child with DD), B represents the family's resources, C represents the family's definition of the event, and X represents the "crisis". Later versions of the model added other variables in an attempt to describe the process of adaptation over time.

The work of Rappoport (1963) had identified potential crisis periods for families of the child with special needs. Some of them which are relevant for this chapter are :

At diagnosis

- When the parents realize the implications of the impairment for the child and family.
- When a decision about placement is to be made (hospital, school etc.).
- When a decision about future pregnancies have to be made.
- During subsequent pregnancies.
- When the prospect of promotion or job change involves moving away from family, neighbourhood and professional supports.
- When the child with special needs goes to primary school, and when he would have changed to senior school, had he/she not been disabled.
- If there is significant deterioration in the disorder, so that it becomes life threatening or terminal.
- If the child dies.
- When the child fails to negotiate a normal development stage (talking, walking, reading etc.).
- If another child fails in the family, develops the same or another disorder.
- At the onset of puberty.
- When leaving school and starting work.
- If the child requires surgery(ies).
- If the child goes into residential care.

Families differ in their responses to stressful events, such as mentioned above. There has, however, been an interesting study on the role played by Factor C, perceptions, in the process of adaption by the families.

Besides the definition of stressful events, Factor C might also include a cognitive reappraisal of the situation to make it more manageable or to maintain an optimistic outlook or acceptance. Mullins (1987) had cited many examples of cognitive reappraisal which are present in many parent-written manuscripts that describe how their lives have been enriched and made more meaningful because of having parented their child with special needs. There is another important dimension which could help in family adaptation to child with exceptionality; the family resources. According to Farber (1975), the extent of family resources affects its function. Abrams and Kaslow (1977) have also noted that families with limited resources are less able to redirect their resources to service needs.

A Model of Stress in Families of Children with Developmental Disabilities

There are, according to Perry (2004), a number of significant limitations to these family stress models and the way they are typically used in research on families of children with Developmental Disabilities (DD). First, the X factor is inappropriately conceptualized as a crisis or even as adaptation (xX) to a crisis or stressful life event, as is often assumed. This does not appear to be the only or most helpful assumption to make regarding families of children with DD. Second, there is considerable confusion between Perception and Stressor Event in studies using these models. Are parent reports of child difficulty part of A (the stressor) or the meaning they attribute to the stressor (C)? Meaning, in a deeper existential sense, is not typically studied, and if it were it is likely that it would differ across individuals in the family. Third, the B or bB factor is excessively broad and needs to be broken down much more specifically. It includes new and old resources of the family, but does not make the crucial distinction between individual resources of parent(s) such as beliefs and coping styles *versus* family system resources such as cohesion and family harmony. Furthermore, it does not separate these within family resources from social supports and professional services received from outside the family. More fundamentally, there is the issue of whether a family or individual model is most useful. These models purport to be family models, but typically individual measures are used to operationalize the domains. Finally, the very recent versions of this model are so elaborate, including a number of variables that cannot be readily measured, that they are of dubious practical utility in applied research. Hence, he developed a model of stress in families of developmentally disabled children.

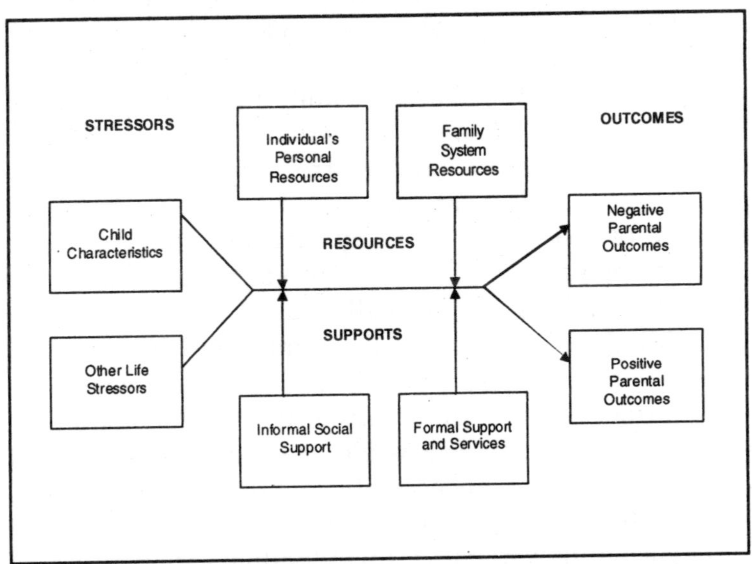

Figure 2.5 : A model of stress in families of children with Developmental Disabilities

Source : Perry (2004)

The model (shown in Figure 2.5) includes four major components: Stressors, Resources, Supports, and Outcomes, each of which is divided into two domains. Stressors are the major and minor stressful stimuli in the life of parents of children with DD, including those associated with the child, as well as other life stressors. These could be dependency in self-help tasks, cognitive or developmental level, frequency and severity of maladaptive behaviour, diagnosis or type of DD, age, and gender. There could be 'Other Life Stressors' too which are faced by other families as well like those related to employment, those pertaining to illness in other family members, financial problems, and so on.

The Resources area consists of the personal resources of the individual parent(s) and family resources. Individual's Personal Resources consist of personality variables and cognitive coping strategies and beliefs, as well as demographic factors. Family System Resources are comprised variables that tap family functioning, marital satisfaction, and demographic variables (such as SES and marital status). The family stress literature and the theoretical models mentioned earlier look at the family as the unit of analysis, as do many clinicians taking a family systems perspective. However, in empirical studies, the family variables are typically based on one or more individuals' perception of the family and it is unclear whether these really differ from individual variables. Furthermore, there are a substantial number of single parents, for whom these variables may not make sense, and research has not necessarily addressed this reality sufficiently. In future research, efforts should be made to untangle family variables from individual variables as well as, in couples, marital from family variables, if possible. In the present model, these marital and/or family measures are considered as independent variables not outcome measures, as outcomes are conceived of as necessarily individual variables.

The third major component of the model consists of the Supports the parent or family may receive from outside the immediate family, from informal social networks and from formal support services. Informal Social Support is emotional sustenance and/or tangible help actually received and/or perceived to be available from extended family members, friends, neighbours, social organizations, and religious communities. Formal supports and services are professional or paraprofessional interventions; including education/treatment programmes for the child with DD and family interventions such as individual, marital, or family counselling, respite care, behaviour management training, parent support groups, and parents' organizations.

The Outcomes in the model, in keeping with the "resource imbalance" tradition, may be thought of as what is left over after considering the primarily negative (but also potentially positive) impact of the Stressors, mediated and/or moderated by the primarily positive (but also potentially negative) influences of the various Resources and Supports available. This residual quantity consists of emotional states and cognitive appraisals and attributions about those emotional states, and can be positive and/or negative (ibid).

These models have given a theoretical perspective to the experiential stress and coping of the families of children with exceptionalities. The researchers have steadily refined and elaborated the classical ABCX model to account for a number of other factors contributing to familial stress. The chapter now moves from an adaptive response of the families to a situational understanding of response to disability. The family systems model shall provide a theoretical basis for this understanding.

The Family System Model

Modern systems theories about families have been derived from General Systems Theories (GST). System theorists endeavour to explain behaviour of complex, organized systems of all sorts. GST is considered by some scholars as a 'unique worldview' rather than a theory, which requires adopting "systems thinking". System thinking requires one to look at the world where the objects are interrelated with one another.

Von Bertanlanffy (1975a:159) defined systems as, "set of elements standing in interrelation among themselves and with the environment". GST made way to the families through Psychiatry (Gray *et al.*, 1969). Many psychiatrists began thinking of families as systems, thus laying the foundation for family therapy. Gradually, GST made its presence felt in sociology and then in family social sciences.

There are three core assumptions of system theories :

- *Systems theories could unify sciences:* it is argued by system theorists whether a system contains individual in a family or programming units in a computer system, there are some basic principles which could be applicable to both.
- *Systems could be understood as a whole rather than in component parts:* the famous Gestalt's concept of wholeness (or non-summavity) that is, "the whole is greater than sum of its parts". Wholeness is the characteristic of systems because there are properties or behaviours of the system that do not derive from the component parts themselves when considered in isolation. These are called Emergents as they emerge only at the systemic level.
- *Human systems are unique in their self reflexivity:* "Human systems are characterized by their self reflexivity, that is, by their ability to make themselves and their own behaviour the object of examination and the target of explanation" (p. 329). Self reflexivity is also what allows human beings to examine their systems and establish goals for themselves.

There are three main domains which had been identified where the system approaches excel in asking and answering questions about families.

1. *Understanding the family processes:* When the family is described as a system then the system theories could be used to understand intra-family process - such as family functioning, family communication and transactional patterns, family conflict, separateness and connectedness among members, cohesion, integration and adaptation to change through transactions among family members. The family processes could be understood as the product of the entire system, shifting the primary focus away from the individual family member to relationships among the members of the family system.
2. *Relationship of the Family System to other Systems :* There is another important property of the system known as hierarchy, which allows the theorists to acknowledge systems at other levels beside the level of a family unit. When systems smaller to that of family are considered, they are called subsystems and systems larger than the family system are called suprasystems. Both these systems allow the family scientists to explore questions in greater depths than would have been possible by mechanistic approaches.
3. *Changes in the family systems :* These system theories have been used to describe structural changes in the family system, a process which has been called morphogenesis. The minor structural changes among system's components, such as when family members modify their individual behaviours, are termed as the first order change. This change does not have the ability to modify/alter the system though it may render it vulnerable to relapse. The change which is a higher level of change could alter the system and theorists refer to it as the second-order change.

Concepts of the Family System Theory (cited in Whitchurch and Constantine, 1993).

Interdependence/Mutual Influence

System has been looked at as a set of interrelationships or it is set of components. The latter is useful for conceptualization of family systems where the components of the system are the individual family members. The interdependence of the component also signifies mutual influence on behaviour of the components. In familial context, it means that the behaviour of one member would affect every other member.

Hierarchy

Hierarchy has been used to describe the GST's perception of nature as a "layering" of systems of increasing complexity: subsystems, systems and suprasystems. For instance, the sibling subsystem is located within the family system which in turn part of the community suprasystem, a nation suprasystem and so on. Miller (1978) referred to these layers as "echelons". In families, hierarchy often associates itself with power. A parental subsystem for instance could be seen as higher echelon than an offspring subsystem, exercising parental authority over the latter.

Boundaries and Open/Closed Systems

Boundary is a vital concept in the systems theory. A boundary would delineate what is part of the system and what is not. Boundaries mark the interface between the system and the environment. The environment may be called as a suprasystem as in the ecological perspective. The observer's judgement assumes great importance while determining the boundary of any system. There is certain degree of subjectivity involved when the observer delineates any system. Boundaries of any systems are also characterized by permeability; a quality which would determine the degree to which the flow of matter, energy and information is permitted in the system. The extreme condition which is termed impermeability; which does not allow any exchange and amorphous/transparent; which offer no impediment to such interchange. The two extremities are impossible in cases of family systems which are classified as open systems with varying degree of openness.

The concept of boundary is operationalized in one of the either ways - (i) by an assessment of permeability or of the inverse, the internal cohesion of the family (the degree of involvement) (Constantine, 1986); and (ii) by emotional connectedness among family members (Olson *et al.*, 1979). The concept of boundary also features between the subsystems within the systems like the parental and the sibling system.

Equifinality

Open systems are characterized by the systems concept of equifinality, or the ability of the system to achieve the same goals through different routes (von Bertalanffy, 1968). Equifinality could very well be observed in family systems as well. Consider a family having a goal to educate their child with special needs upto College level. The family may utilize the available resources in the family to achieve this or take a bank loan for fulfilling their family ambition. It, therefore, does not matter which path is adopted for realizing the final aim.

Feedback and Control

"A feedback loop is a closed circuit, or path, along which information could be traced from one point in a system, through one or more other parts of the system or its environment, and back to the point of origin". Such a system is capable of maintaining its own behaviour as the information entering the loop is transformed and ultimately fed back into the loop. There could be two kinds of feedback:

1. *Negative feedback:* Where the system endeavours to maintain a condition of dynamic equilibrium, a state

known as homeostasis. According to Galvin and Brommel (1991), in case of a family the negative feedback loop operates when the members try to maintain the family's transactional patterns so as to maintain their sense of balance even if that balance is dysfunctional.

2. *Positive feedback:* When the deviation in the system is amplified or result in more variation in system behaviour, they are called positive feedback loop. When applied to family system, it would mean changing of overall behaviour of members.

Modelling the Theory

After defining all the important and relevant concepts of the systems theory, the chapter would attempt to model this theory in relation to the child with special needs in the family. Figures 2.6 a and b endeavour to represent the dynamic nature of a system in two dimensional space by showing system change through diagramming reorganization of a fictional family at two different stages. Figure 2.6 a represents the arrangement of the system, components, prior to the disclosure of their younger child's disability. The family consists of father, mother and two children; the younger one is developmentally disabled. The father is shown to be more distanced from the child subsystem. The subsystems have permeable boundaries. The family system is embedded in the suprasystems of the parents' and the children's respective circle of friends and the community. The suprasystemic level also includes the environment with which the family transact; that is, everything external to their family system. Figure 2.6b depicts when the state of the family system when the members are acquainted with the fact about the disability of their younger child. The changes which occur at the systemic level are depicted through thickening of the boundaries resulting in impermeability. The subsystemic boundaries are shown to be in transition, which shows the changing relationships in the family. The family may become temporarily dysfunctional until they find means to attain their new homeostatic state.

In this segment, there was an attempt to present a model using the systems assumptions and concepts presented earlier in the chapter. This was an example to show these concepts and assumptions could be used to describe or study any family, regardless of family form. It may however be imperative and interesting to note how the special needs of the child interface with the family thus, bringing about a change in the system which may disrupt the equilibrium.

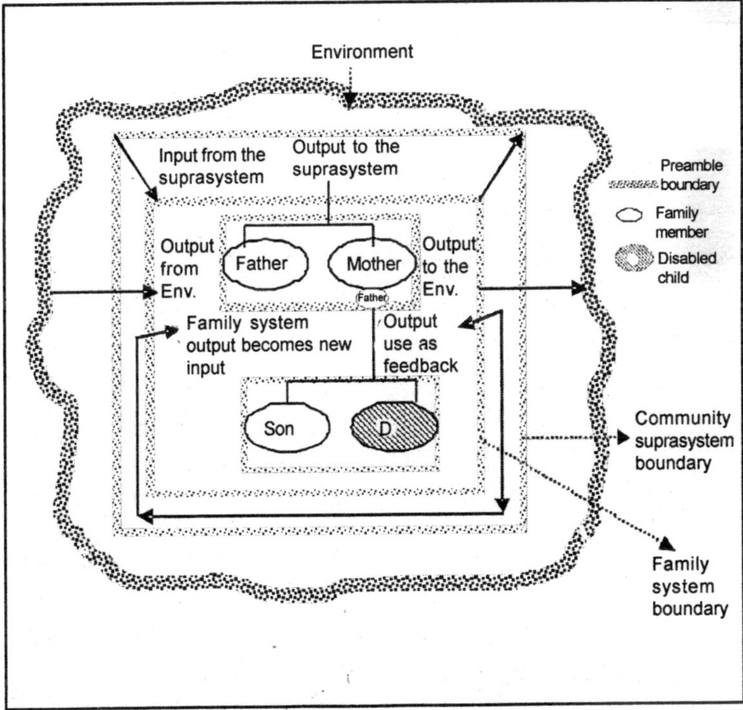

Figure 2.6a: Homeostatic state of the family : Disability status of the child unknown adapted and modified from : Whitchurch and Constantine (1993 : 338)

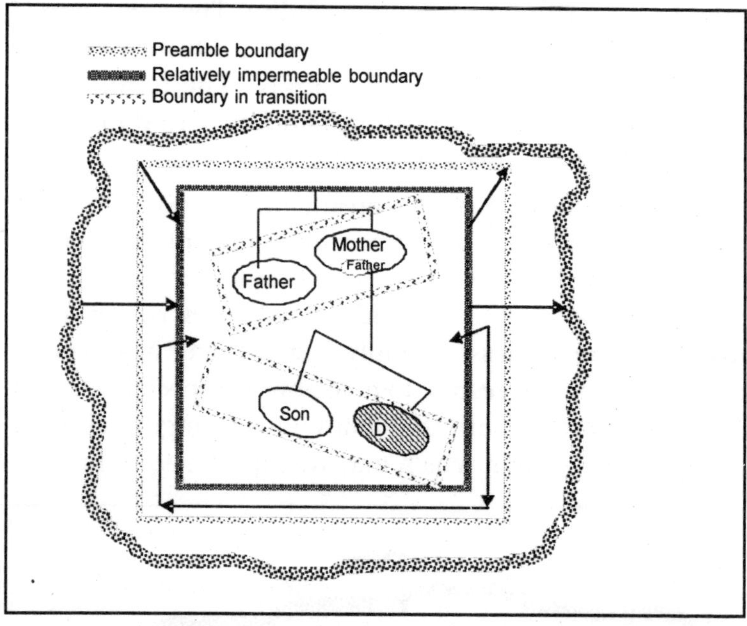

Figure 2.6b: Dysfunctional state of the family immediately after diagnosis of the child's disability

The diagrammatic interface between the family system and the child's disability is shown in Figure 2.7. From the family point of view, family systems theory must first include the disability system in its thinking. Disability cannot be constructed solely using the biological criterion to meet the medical needs. Figure 2.7 attempts a different classification scheme which would provide a better linkage between biological and psychosocial worlds and thereby, clarify the relationship between disability and family. The illness model that has applied to families giving children with special needs endorses the notion that illness (implies disability here) becomes incorporated into the family system and all its and illness-specific family dynamics such as communication, problem solving, hierarchy, role allocation, affective involvement, social support, utilization and community resources and home based medical care.

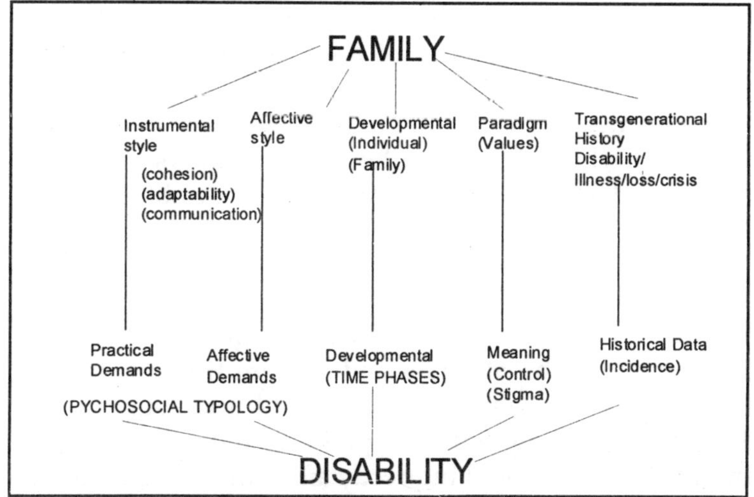

Figure 2.7: Interface between the disability and the family.

Source : Adapted and Modified from Rolland (1988:18).

Disability certainly places some additional practical and affective demands on the family members. The instrumental and affective style of the family shall determine how well it is able to cater to the practical and emotional demands of the child with special needs. The interaction between disability and family's development is also very crucial to understand. At every stage, the family has to deal with certain developmental tasks, successful achievement of which leads to satisfaction and success with later tasks. Families with disabled children often experience renewed sorrow, apprehension and stress when they fail to achieve their familial goals of children meeting the normal milestones. All families as systems adopt a value orientation, belief system which shapes the behaviour patterns towards common problems. The value system may determine a particular treatment compliance, certain health behaviour and family preferences about participating in the child's medical procedures, social behaviour etc. It may be important to know family's beliefs about the etiology of the disability. Families may often attribute this to prior misdeeds, blaming other members (genetics) or simply bad luck. The trans-generational history of how the family had fared during an earlier crisis or loss would also affect the family's stance on dealing with disability. These were the familial attributes which determine how the members deal with disability. They are certain dimensions of disability which impact the family's response. The psychosocial typology is created on the basis of the onset, course, outcome and degree of disability. Each phase of managing disability has its different psychosocial tasks which require significantly different strengths, attitudes and changes from the family. The societal and familial meaning and understanding of the disability along with the previous data on incidence and progression would indirectly affect the response of the family towards the child with disability.

From a systems perspective, it was important to know how disability interacts with the family to produce actions and responses towards the need of the child having a disability. The disability of one child has an effect on the development of all members and family. This discussion clarified conceptual thinking about the system created at the interface of disability with the family. The chapter would now move on to look at the social ecology framework in relation to the families of disabled children.

Social Ecology Model

Bronfenbrenner's ecological contexts (Figure 2.8) offer a framework that enables us to simultaneously consider what is taking place within the immediate household (microsystem), the forces at work in the larger social system in which the family is functioning (exosystem), the interaction of these settings with one another (mesosystem), and the overriding cultural beliefs and values that influence the microsystem and exosystems (macrosystem). These contexts operate independently, and the nature of this interdependence changes over time (Lerner and Spanier, 1978 cited in Shea and Bauer, 1991).

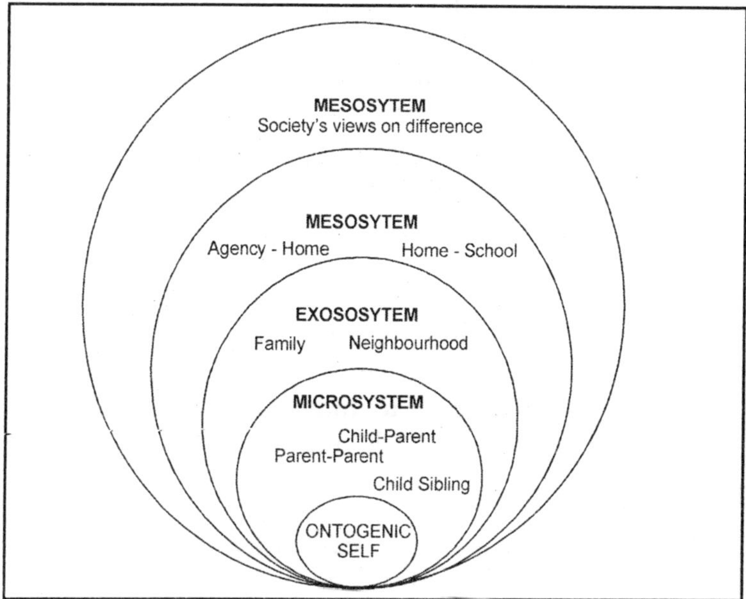

Figure 2.8 : Developmental Contexts as Related to Parent and Family Adaptation

Source: Shea and Bauer 1991: 25.

According to Bronfenbrenner (1979:3), development is defined as "a lasting change in the way in which a person perceives and deals with his environment". The ecological environment is conceived as a set of nested structures, each inside the next. At the innermost level of the ecological schema, one of the basic units of analysis is a dyad, or two persons system. Several findings indicate that the capacity of the dyad to serve as an effective context for human development is crucially dependent on the presence and participation of third parties, such as spouses, relatives and friends and neighbours. If such third parties are absent, or if they play a disruptive rather than supportive role, the developmental process, considered as a system, breaks down like a three-legged stool, it is more easily broken or shorter than the others. The same triadic principle applies to relations between settings. Thus the capacity of a setting-such as the home, school, or workplace - to function effectively as a context for development is seen to depend on the existence and nature of social interconnections between settings including joint participation, communication, and the existence of information in each setting about the other (ibid, 5-6).

If the developmental contexts (Figure 2.8) were elaborated, there would be better clarity on how these relate to parents and families of children with special needs. A clear definition of the terminologies such as the ontogenic self, microsystem, exosystem, mesosystem and macrosystem would be essential in order to understand the implications of these structures on the child and the family.

The Ontogenic System

The ontogenic system was not a component of Bronfenbrenner's theory but was postulated by Kurdek (1981). The ontogenic system includes the individual's personal and psychological competencies for dealing with stress. It represents what an individual brings to the family setting and the parenting role. Personal characteristics like gender, demographic characteristics, nature of child's exceptionality have been explored in various research studies.

Mothers and fathers cope differently with the emotional distress caused to their child's exceptionality. Studies have noted that fathers were less distressed, displayed higher self-esteem and more locus of control than mothers of children of special needs (Holroyd, 1974; Goldberg *et al.*, 1986). This could be attributed to mothers spending more time with the children and being burdened with the additional care demands. However, Cummings (1976) hypothesized that fathers contrary to mothers of children with special needs had fewer opportunities to do something directly helpful to the child which shows their concern towards their children. Gray (2003) found that mothers and fathers differed greatly in terms of the impact created by their child's autism. The mothers were found to be severely affected by their child's condition and concerned about his/her dependency. On the contrary, the fathers acknowledged that their child's condition did not affect them personally though they noted that the child's autism had presented severe difficulties for their families.

Darling (1979:47-51) studied certain parental traits that may affect acceptance of the child with exceptionalities like -

- *Social class* : Parents of lower socioeconomic status appear to be more accepting than parents of higher status.
- *Parent's personal self-acceptance* : The parents' level of personal self-acceptance appears to be directly related to their capacity to accept the child.
- *Parents' age* : Older and experienced parents might be able to adapt better. The younger parents however, might have an advantage in having an opportunity to bear other (normal) children.
- *Prior experience with children* : Prior experience with normal and with exceptional children appears to facilitate acceptance.
- *Reason for having children* : If the parents expect their children to have certain qualities such as a particular sex, physical attractiveness, intelligence or athletic ability or to play a specific role in family life, then the acceptance level for their child with special needs would be low.

There is enough research evidence about the effect of nature of child's exceptionality on ability of parents to cope with stress. A study conducted by Irvin, Kennel and Klaus (1982) indicated that parental reactions to their child with disability depend on characteristics of the disability. Table 2.1 presents the characteristics of the disability, which affect the parental reactions.

Table 2.1. Characteristics Impacting on Parents' Reactions to their Child's Handicapping Condition

Is the handicap correctable?

Is the handicap visible?

Is the handicap impacting the central nervous system?

Is the handicap life threatening?

Is the handicap impacting on future development?

Is the handicap affecting genitalia?

Is the handicap evident in a single sign or in multiple signs?

Is the handicap familial

Is the handicap requiring repeated hospitalization, physicals or visits to the agencies?

Source: Adapted from Irvin, Kennel and Klaus 1982 (cited in Shea and Bauer 1991:29).

Thus it may be concluded looking at the table that the parental reactions and stress depends on the type and severity of the disability. There are however contradictory studies available which indicate that parental stress is primarily a function of their personality and physiology and not a consequence of the nature of child's disability (see Bradshaw, 1978).

The Microsystem

Bronfenbrenner (1979) had defined microsystem as "a pattern of activities, roles and interpersonal relations experienced by the developing person in a given setting with particular physical and material characteristics" (p. 22). Microsystem here signifies the nature of interaction among family members. The intrafamilial relationships have been explored in many research studies. The microsystem assumes paramount importance in a child's development. According to Germain and Maisto (1982), the presence of both parents in the home is a great source of emotional support to the family. Drotar *et al.,* (1975) have reported that a satisfactory relationship between the parents is crucial to adaptation to the child's exceptionality. A child with special needs places greater care demands on the mother. In a study conducted by Cantwell, Baker and Rutter (1979) it was found that the mothers spend twice as much time with their children having special needs in concentrated interaction than with their normal children.

Another important aspect of this subsystem is sibling-child relationship. Featherstone (1980) had indicated that siblings of children with special needs perceive themselves as belonging to dual cultures; their normal classmates and their exceptional family. Throughout their lives, these brothers and sisters share many same concerns that parents of children with special needs experience, as well as issues that are uniquely theirs. These concerns are well known to their parents and have been documented in the research and clinical literature. Among the concerns mentioned by authors, parents, and siblings themselves include: feelings of isolation, guilt, resentment, perceived pressure to achieve, increased caregiving demands, and concerns about their role in their sibling's future (The Council for Exceptional Children, 2002). Each child's reaction to having a sibling with a disability will vary depending on his or her age and developmental level. The responses and feelings of the non-disabled sibling towards the sibling with a disability are not likely to be static, but rather tend to change over time as the sibling adapts to having a brother or sister with a disability and copes with day-to-day realities (NICHCY, 1994).

Every relationship is reciprocal. If the child with special needs impacts the parents and family members in the abovementioned ways, their reactions and behaviours would certainly affect the child. Needless to say, that a positive response from the parents and siblings shall have a positive impact on the development of the child.

The Exosystem

The next level has been named exosystem and defined as a system referring to "one or more settings that do not involve the developing person as an active participant, but in which events occur that affect, or are affected by, what happens in the setting containing a developing person" (Bronfenbrenner, 1979:26). Settings within the exosystem may include workplace, neighbourhood, school and community. The presence of a child with special needs would certainly alter the social interaction patterns of the family. McAllister, Butler and Lei (1973) in their study have reported that the parents of children with behavioural disorders were less likely to visit relatives, friends, neighbours and coworkers.

Such poor social interaction patterns could lead to weak external support system. The actors of the exosystem assume paramount importance in case of families having a child with exceptionality as they could be turned into great support systems. It is therefore important for professionals to strengthen these support systems in order to develop resilience in families.

The Mesosystem

A mesosystem comprises the interrelations among two or more settings in which the developing person actively participates (Bronfenbrenner, 1979:25). In the context of the child with special needs it could be home-special/ inclusive school or a service provider-home. "A mesosystem is thus a system of microsystems. It is formed or extended whenever the developing person moves into a new setting" (ibid).

Karnes and Zehrback (1972) suggested that coordinated school-family endeavours serve children with exceptionalities better than school endeavours alone (cited in Shea and Bauer, 1991). School-family involvement could positively lessen the care and educational responsibilities at both ends. McAfee and Vergason (1979) make three recommendations for effective collaboration between the school and home efforts-

- School and family should develop a written or unwritten contract structured to ensure that each contributes towards common goals for the child.
- Parents should assume some responsibility for their child's education.
- School and family should seek ways to regain community support for the educational system.

Thus, it is evident that an effective partnership between agencies like home-special/inclusive school or home-service organization could prove extremely beneficial for the child's development.

The Macrosystem

"A macrosystem refers to consistencies, in the form and content of lower order systems (micro-, meso- , and exo-) that exist, or could exist, at the level of the sub culture or the culture as a whole, along with any belief, systems or ideology underlying such consistencies". (Bronfenbrenner 1979:26). The macrosystem is concerned with the cultural beliefs, values and attitudes surrounding family life and exceptionality in society (Shea and Bauer 1991:38). Riegal (1975) had also suggested that though the development takes place within particular context, an individual's development must be viewed within the context of broad social and cultural change.

The birth of an exceptional child in a family may result in loss of self-esteem, feeling of shame, defensiveness, and loneliness for parents and siblings. This is due to the expectation of the society from families to produce normal and healthy children, failing which a stigma is attached to that particular family. According to Shea and Bauer (1991), it is important that the stigma is managed through managing impressions projected by parent behaviour as well as developing an ideology consistent with cultural beliefs. The professionals working with families of children with special needs must also be aware of their personal assumptions and biases. The acceptance of the family must be open rather than as a stereotyped group.

Another component of the macrosystem is the statutory and non-statutory policies and programmes for the children with special needs and their families. It is a reflection of the underlying ideology regarding the disabled population of any country. General improvements in services for children with disabilities would lead to increasing optimism amongst the children and their families about the feasibility of ordinary adult life experiences and independent living and employment.

This segment explained with the help of systems approach where the family adaptation to the birth of a child with special needs was seen to be affected by series of ecological contexts. Along with the discussion on the preceding models, this model has helped in clarifying and understanding the needs of the families having an exceptional child. The following section on comparison and critique of the models presented in this chapter would explicate the linkages and differences between the models and spell out their utility for practice.

A Synthesis of the Models

In this chapter as all of the theories were intending to explain family behaviour, on the surface they might appear similar. The basic premise of this chapter is that the families are the transmitting agents of basic human competencies to the progeny. Families change and are influenced by its members and the environment. The theories which had been selected and reviewed gave a thorough and a broad understanding of the family of the children with special needs. Out of four reviewed models, the stage theory model was specific to grieving by families at the advent of the birth/diagnosis of the birth of the child with special needs and thereafter but the rest of the models had wider range and implications.

The ecological approach to study of families may be classified as most broad-based for it includes family, peers, neighbourhood and community, service agencies and State which seem to impact the child. Every theory includes the notion of time in some way. According to White and Klein (1996), "Theories may be placed on a continuum between static and dynamic based on the extent to which they incorporate time as an important concept". The presence or absence of an explicit reference to a process that is time dependent in the theory has been used as a criterion to differentiate between static and dynamic by them. For instance, the stage theory incorporates time dependencies through transition or stages of grieving. In systems theory, the recursive nature of successive feedback loop suggests dependency on time. The family stress models do not have an explicit reference and so are the social ecology models. This however, does not mean that they could be classified as static as according to Collins (1988:387), every theory in social sciences specifies or at least implies some time scale which may range from seconds to centuries. Therefore, it may be wiser to classify it under three time scales instead of static and dynamic: episodic time, lifetime and historic time. In this perspective, stage theory would be classified as lifetime, family systems and stress theory as episodic and ecological theory as historical time oriented.

"All families change over time, but theories approach change in a myriad of ways (White and Klein, 1996:250)". How the families change can be another standard for comparison of the presented models. It may be interesting to note whether these models envision the source of change within the family or external to the family unit. Let us attempt to distinguish the four theories discussed here according to the primary focus of change. The stage theory model talks about the family going through the stages of grieving. One stage may lead to the other depending upon the nature of the family. The source of change could then be considered as endogenous. System theories, because they incorporate several levels on which the change may take place are either endogenous or exogenous, but usually both. Ecological theories take the process of adaptation to the environment as basic process of change. Because adaptation carries with it the connotation of a unit adapting to its changing environment, the source of change would come from outside of the family unit. The family stress models consider coping as a change in the family which could be brought about by a number of interacting factors which could be internal or external, therefore, the family stress models like the systems model could have endogenous or exogenous sources of change.

All these theories have implications for intervention. Each theory in its own way gives some clues about what kind of change is required, how to do it and what are the consequences likely to be. All theories discussed in the chapter have been contextualized to families of children with special needs and all of them point towards the probable intervention areas. A theoretical understanding leads to a better needs assessment of the families. The stage theory models could be utilized with families to help assess their level of adjustment and to propose an intervention based on their emotional readiness to receive additional services (O'Hara, Chaiklin and Mosher, 1980; Thompson and Young, 1977). For instance families undergoing the shock and denial have to be helped to come to terms with reality, or those who have accepted the child's disability may be amenable to prescriptive and informative counselling. The Family Stress Models indicate the interacting factors that produce stress and look at how families cope or adapt to the stress or crisis.

These models have been the basis of various intervention models for dealing with stress. For instance, Harris, *et al.*, (1991) summarized the two major models of dealing with stress for parents of autistic children: instrumental and palliative strategies. Instrumental strategies (i.e., parents education, information programmes) focus on empowering parents to implement change in the person or the environment. Palliative strategies, such as self-help groups, enable parents to tolerate stress through internal mechanisms. The Family System Models are increasingly being used to address problems which were once looked at only from an individual's standpoint. The family system theory has proved extremely useful in the area of family therapy, in guiding intervention and interpreting complex relationships between individuals and their families. The Social Ecology Models offer some interesting prospects for studying individual family members, the family as a group, and the general ecological context in which those groups function. It provides the practitioner with a wider perspective of the interacting systems and intervention at various levels including the outermost macro level. It is imperative to understand the prevailing culture and ideology of segregation of children with special needs which must pave way to rights based approaches and their inclusion in the society. This could be made possible through advocacy for formulation of policies and programmes which provide equal opportunity to all its citizens irrespective of their abilities.

This part of the chapter attempted to compare the models and synthesize them to develop a comprehensive understanding and their implications in the intervention arena. The next segment would look at some research responses in India so as to get an idea of how these family processes have been studied in the country in relation to families of children with special needs and to suggest some future directions in research.

Research Responses in India

Research on families having disabled members has been reviewed with reference to the following aspects (Kashyap 1991:273-281):

1. *The effect on the family of the presence of a disabled individual:* She has cited seven studies where the researchers have focused on the effect of presence of disabled children. She noted that very little and very limited research has been done on disabled children and their families.
2. *The influencing factors within the family:* Of the fourteen research studies she had referred dealing with this aspect; twelve studied only the attitudes of the parents towards their disabled children as the influencing factors.
3. *The family's coping strategies:* Only one research has been reported in her review in the important area of coping by families. Gandotra (1985) studies the ways and means used by twenty-five home makers to cope with the problems arising from the presence of disabled individual in the family (cited in Kashyap, 1991).
4. *Professional intervention for helping the family to cope* : In this category seven studies were reviewed that reflected that professionals had emphasized on families of the mentally challenged children and that too on educational programmes for training parents in behaviour modification techniques.

The research review of families with disabled individuals by Kashyap suggests that families of the mentally challenged children have received more attention by the researchers as compared to the other disabilities. Also, some very important areas like coping and adaptation by the families, interventions other than education and training, influencing factors within the families apart the parental attitudes towards their disabled children, sibling relationships need consideration by the researchers.

"Research in understanding of families and working with the families in the true sense is still eluding Indian scene" (Peshawaria *et al.,* 1995:12). More often than not the emphasis is on the epidemiological aspects. Major focus of the studies has been studying the attitudes of parents towards their children with special needs and the disability, which has received the maximum attention of the researchers, is mental retardation.

Prabhu (1970) studied the need of parents in terms of reasons for institutional placement. Impact on the parents was studied by Seshadri *et al.,* (1983), Wig *et al.,* (1985), Sethi and Sitholey (1986), Sequiera *et al.,* (1990), Tangri and Verma (1992). A study investigating social emotional support for parents was presented by Moudgil *et al.,* (1985); treatment seeking behaviour of parents (Chaturvedi and Malhotra, 1982); consumer demand of services by parents (Peshawaria and Venkatesan); and parents needs was presented from a conceptual framework by Pehawaria and Menon in 1991 (cited in Peshawaria *et al.,* 1995).

There has been limited literature on family's response to the child with special needs in context to our country. Given the importance of the institution of family in India and its effect on the developing child, research and practice with families' gains paramount importance. Presence of a child with special needs affect the family functions and processes in a number of ways. It is important to understand these underlying processes theoretically and establish them empirically so as to initiate some positive action for development of family systems.

Conclusion

Family, with all its content and its roles, could be described as a fundamental human union in which life begins and ends. Children born in a family have the right to the care and protection not only of the adult family members but of the siblings and community as well. From the time of the child's birth, the family is the one who has direct, intensive, positive and negative influences on the child's development as a person (especially in childhood and adolescence). Introducing a child to culture, values and norms of society begins in one's family. Therefore, for the harmonious and complete development of a child's personality and self-esteem, its learning of all necessary life skills and appropriate behaviour, the natural, happy, loving and understanding family environment is vital. The circumstances are not any different for the child with special needs in a family. They need as much affection and care as the non-disabled children. Every member of a system influences every other member in a circular chain reaction. A family system is constantly changing as children develop; thus it is almost impossible to know for certain causes of particular behaviours in children. The family environment must be stress-free for the ensuring overall and healthy development of all its children.

The chapter has endeavoured to feature the psychosocial responses of the families to the children with special need's. The chapter explored four theoretical models which have guided research and intervention in this area. It moved from models which focused on micro issues of parental reactions and adjustment to the child with special needs to the models which explicated the environmental effects on families. The explored theories facilitated the understanding of the family systems and provoked a thought on its practical implications for families having children with special needs.

The discussion and understanding led to some concerns to be borne in mind while intervening at the family level. The key issues in working with families of the children with special needs have been summarized by Wall (2004:44-45) with focus on autistic children:

- the sensitive nature of the issues the practitioners are dealing with;

- the impact individual family members have on the child with special needs;
- the dynamic and evolving nature of the family;
- functioning abilities of the family as a whole;
- the individual perspectives of family members;
- the need to support the family members;
- the existing support networks within and outside the family;
- the positive and negative effects of family members on the child with special needs;
- the fact that the family knows the child best;
- our own assessment processes - to ensure that the practitioner considers family issues in an holistic assessment of the child's needs;
- current legislation and guidance related to the child's special need and specifically supporting families of children with special needs;
- the practitioner's own working practices with professionals from other disciplines and agencies; and
- always remember that, whilst the child must remain the focus of the practitioner's work, the family issues must not be ignored.

Bailey *et al.*, (1986) had used a "goodness of fit" concept (between family, child, and services provided), suggesting a functional approach in assessing family needs and goals, and implementing and evaluating services. They see four, main overarching goals of family centred intervention as: incorporating family coping assistance, offering better understanding of child development, promoting enhanced parent-child interactions, and relating to parents as equal partners with professionals in the planning, implementation and evaluation of services.

Dunst *et al.* (1988) offered a detailed and eloquent model of family centered intervention in childhood disability. They argue that the first duty of professionals is not to meet family needs, but to help families become more competent to meet their own needs. Their approach emphasizes that professional intervention should not dwell on deficits and seek to fix problems, but should build on family strengths and enhance positive problem solving. To this, Dunst *et al.*, identified three realms of information that are fundamental to inform professional help giving: an understanding of the needs and aspirations of family members, an appreciation of the family functioning style, and finally, a knowledge of the existing and potential support and resources that are available to the family through formal and informal sources in their community networks.

Thus, it may be concluded that an insight into these theoretical models is extremely vital for chalking out intervention strategies and devising research methodologies for understanding and working with families having children with special needs. The chapter attempted to review and contextualize these theoretical perspectives in order to develop a meaningful holistic perspective for researchers and practitioners in the field.

References

Bailey, Jr., D. B., R. J. Simeonsson, P. J. Winton, G. S. Huntington, M. Isbell P. Comfort, K. J. O'Donnell, & J. M. Helm (1986). Family-focused intervention: A functional model for planning, implementing, and evaluating services in early intervention. *Journal of the Division for Early Childhood*, 19, 156-171.

Bertalanffy, L. Von (1975). *Perspectives on General System Theory: Scientific-philosophical Studies*. New York: George Braziller.

Blacher, J. (1984). A dynamic perspective on the impact of severely handicapped child on the family. In Jan Blacher (Ed.), *Severely Handicapped Young Children and Their Families: Research in Review*. Orlando, Florida: Academic Press.

Blacher, J. (1984). Sequential stages of parental adjustment to the birth of child with handicaps: Fact or artifact? *Mental Retardation*, 22, 55-68.

Black, Dora (1982). Handicap and family therapy. In Arnon Bentovim, Gill Gorell Barnes and Alan Cooklin (Eds.) *Family Therapy: Complementary Frameworks of Theory and Practice* Volume 2. London: Academic Press.

Boss, Pauline (1987). Family Stress. In Marvin B. Sussman and Suzanne K. Steinmetz (Eds.) *Handbook of Marriage and Family*. New York: Plenum Press.

Bradshaw, J. (1978). Tracing the Causes of Stress in Families with Handicapped Children. *The British Journal of Social Work* 8: 181-192.

Bristol, M. M. (1987). Mothers of children with autism or communication disorders: Successful adaptation and the Double ABCX model. *Journal of Autism and Developmental Disorders*, 17, 469-486.

Bronfenbrenner, Urie (1979). *The Ecology of Human Development: Experiments by Nature and Design*. Cambridge: Harvard University.

Bronfenbrenner, Urie (1986). Ecology of the Family as a Context for Human Development: Research Perspectives. *Developmental Psychology*, 22, 723-742.

Cantwell, D.P., L. Baker and M. Rutter (1979). Families of Autistic and Dysphasic Children: Family Life and Interaction Patterns. *Archives of General Psychiatry* 36(6): 682-87.

Darling, R.B. (1979). *Families Against Society*. Beverly Hills, Calif: Sage.

DeMarco Rosanna, Marliyn Ford-Gilboe, Marie-Luise Friedemann, Hamilton I. McCubbin and Marilyn A.McCubbin (2000). Stress, Coping and Family Health. In Virginia Hill Rice (Ed.). *Handbook of Stress, Coping and Health: Implications of Nursing Research, Theory and Practice*. Thousand Oaks: Sage Publications.

Dickman, I., & S. Gordon (1985). *One miracle at a time: How to get help for your disabled child - from the experience of other parents*. New York: Simon and Schuster.

Drotar, D., A. Baskiewicz, N. Irvin, J. Kennel and M. Klauss (1975). The Adaptations of Parents to the Birth of an Infant with Congenital Malformation. *Paediatrics* 56:710-17.

Duis, S., Summers, M. and C.R. Summers (1997). Parent Versus Child Stress in Diverse Family Types: A Ecological Approach. *Topics in Early Childhood Special Education*, 17, 53-73.

Dunst, C. J., Trivette, C. M., & Deal, A. G. (1988). *Enabling and Empowering Families*. Cambridge, MA: Brookline.

Farber, B. (1975). Family Adoptions to Severally Mentally Retarded Children. In M. Begab and S. Richardson (Eds.). *The Mentally Retarded in Society: A Social Science Perspective*. Baltimore: University Park Press 247-66.

Featherstone, H. (1980). *A difference in the family: Life with a disabled child*. New York: Basic Books, Inc.

Ferguson, Philip M. (2001). Mapping the Family: Disability Studies and the Exploration of Parental Response to Disability. In Gary L. Albrecht, Katherine D. Seelman and Michael Bury (Eds.), *Handbook of Disability Studies*. Thousand Oaks (Cal.): Sage Publications.

Gallimore, R., J. Coots, T. Weisner, H. Garnier, and D. Guthrie (1996). Family Responses to Children with early Developmental Disabilities: II. Accommodation Intensity and Activity in Early and Middle Childhood. *American Journal of Mental Deficiency*, 89, 111-123.

Germain, M.L. and A.A Maisto (1982). The Relationship of a Perceived Family Support System to the Institutional Placement of Mentally Retarded Children. *Education and Training of the Mentally Retarded* 17: 17-33.

Gray, D.E. (2003). Gender and coping: the parents of children with high functioning autism. *Social Science and Medicine*, 56:631-642.

Gray, W.N., F.D. Duhl, and N.D. Rizzo (1969). *General Systems Theory and Psychiatry*. Boston: Little Brown.

Greer, B.G. (1975). On Being the Parent of the Handicapped Child. *Exceptional Children* 41:519.

Gupta, Ashum and Nidhi Singhal (2004). Positive Perceptions in Parents of Children with Disabilities. Asia Pacific Disability Rehabilitation Journal, Vol. 15, No. 1, 22-33.

Harris, S. L., Gill, M. J., & Alessandri, M. (1991). The family with an autistic child. In M. Seligman (Ed.), *The family with a handicapped child* (pp. 269-294). Needham Heights, MA: Allyn & Bacon.

Hartman, A., & J. Laird (1983). *Family-centered Social Work Practice*. New York: Free Press.

Hauser-Cram Penny and Angela Howell (2003). Disability and Development. In Richard M. Lerner, M. Ann Easterbrooks and Jayanthi Mistry (Eds.). *Handbook of Psychology Volume 6 Developmental Psychology* (pp. 513-533). Hoboken, New Jersy: John Wiley and Sons.

Havens, C. Amber (2005). Becoming a Resilient Family: Child Disability and the Family System. *Access Today*, Spring 2005 - Special Volume, Issue 17.

Karnes, M.B., and R.R. Zehrback (1972). Flexibility in Getting Parents Involved in School. *Teaching Exceptional Children* 5(1): 6-19.

Kashyap, L. (1991). Research on families with disabled individuals: review and implications. In Murli Desai (Ed.), *Research on Families with Problems in India*, Volume II. Mumbai: Tata Institute of Social Sciences.

Kubler-Ross, Elizabeth (1969). *On Death and Dying*, New York: MacMillan Publishing Co.

Kurdek, L.A. (1981). An Integrative Perspective on Children's Divorce Adjustment. *American Psychology* 36 (8): 856-77.

McAfee, J.K. and G.A. Vergason (1979). Parent Involvement in the process of special education: Establishing the new partnerships. *Focus on Exceptional Children* 11(2): 1-15.

McAllister, R.L., E.W. Butler and T.P. Lei (1973). Patterns of Social Interaction among the families of behaviorally retarded children. *Journal of Marriage and Family* 35: 359-370.

McCubbin, H.I., & M.A. McCubbin (1988). Typologies of Resilient Families: Emerging Roles of Social Class and Ethnicity. *Family Relations*, 37, 247-254.

McCubbin, M.A. & H.I. McCubbin (1993). Family coping with health crises: The resiliency model of family stress, adjustment and adaptation. In C. Danielson, B. Hamel-Bissell, & P. Winstead-Fry (Eds.), *Families, Health, and Illness*. New York: Mosby.

McCubbin, M.A., & H.I. McCubbin (1996). Resiliency in families: A conceptual model of family adjustment and adaptation in response to stress and crises. In H.I. McCubbin, A.I. Thompson, & M.A. McCubbin (1996). *Family assessment: Resiliency, coping and adaptation--Inventories for research and practice* (pp. 1-64). Madison, WI: University of Wisconsin System.

McKenry, Patrick C. and Sharon J. Price (2000). Families Coping with Problems and Change: A Conceptual Overview. In Patrick C. McKenry and Sharon J. Price (Eds.). *Families & Change: Coping with Stressful Events and Transitions*. Thousand Oaks: Sage Publications Inc.

Mink, I.T., C.E. Meyers and K. Nihira (1983). Taxonomy of Family Life Styles: I. Homes with TMR Children. *American Journal of Mental Deficiency*, 87, 484-497.

Mink, I.T., C.E. Meyers, and K. Nihira (1984). Taxonomy of Family Life Styles: .II. Homes with Slow-learning Children. *American Journal of Mental Deficiency*, 89, 111-123.

Minnes, P. (1988). Family resources and stress associated with having a mentally retarded child. *American Journal on Mental Retardation*, 93, 184-192.

National Information Center For Children and Youth With Disabilities *NICHCY News Digest*, Number 11, 1988 Resources Updated, 1994 Source: http://www.ldonline.org/article/6054 Date of Retrieval: 21st April 2006

O'Hara, D., H. Chaiklin, H. and Mosher, B.S. (1980). A family life cycle plan for delivering services to developmentally handicapped children. *Child Welfare*, 59(2), 80-90.

Perry, Adrienne (2004). A Model of Stress in Families of Children with Developmental Disabilities: Clinical and Research Applications. *Journal on Developmental Disabilities*, Volume 11 Number 1, 1-16.

Peshawaria, Reeta, D.K. Menon, Rahul Ganguly, Sumit Roy, Rajam P.R.S. Pillay and Asha Gupta (1995). *Understanding Indian Families: Having Persons with Mental Retardation*. Secunderabad: National Institute for the Mentally Handicapped.

Riegel, K.F. (1975). Towards a dialectical theory of development. *Human Development* 18: 50-74.

Rolland, John S. (1988). A conceptual model of chronic and life threatening illness and its impact on families. In Catherine S. Chilman, Elam W. Nunnally and Fred M. Cox (Eds.), *Chronic Illness and Disability: Families in Trouble Series*, Volume 2. Newbury Park, Cal.: Sage Publications.

Seligman, M., & Darling, R. B. (1989). *Ordinary families, special children: A systems approach and childhood disability*. New York: Guilford.

The Council for Exceptional Children (2002) *Source*: http://ericec.org/faq/siblings.html Date of Retrieval: 1st July 2006

Thompson, T. and Young, A. (1977). Behavioural counselling of the parents of retarded children. In T. Thompson and J. Grabowski (Eds.), *Behaviour Modification of the Mentally Retarded* (2nd edition). New York: Oxford University Press.

Wall, Kate (2004). *Autism and Early Years Practice: A Guide for Early Years Professionals, Teachers and Parents*. London: Paul Chapman Publishing.

Whitchurch, Gail G. and Larry L. Constantine (1993). Systems Theory. In Pauline G. Boss, William J. Doherty, Ralph LaRossa, Walter R.

Schumm, Suzanne K. Steinmertz (Eds.). *Sourcebook of Family Theories and Methods: A Contextual Approach.* New York: Plenum Press.

White, James M., David M. Klein (1996). *Family Theories: An Introduction.* Thousand Oaks: Sage.

Wikler, L. M. (1986). Family stress theory and research on families of children with mental retardation. In J. J. Gallagher & P. M. Vietze (Eds.), *Families of handicapped persons: Research, programs, and policy issues* (pp. 167-195). Baltimore, MD: Brookes.

Wright, Judith Sewell, Roberta D. Granger and Arnold J. Sameroff (1984). Parental acceptance and developmental handicap. In Jan Blacher (Ed.), *Severely Handicapped Young Children and Their Families: Research in Review*. Orlando, Florida: Academic Press.

3

RIGHTS OF CHILDREN WITH DISABILITY

Introduction

The children with disabilities have always been discriminated against and deprived of the normal activities of the childhood. Throughout history certain basic amenities like education, healthcare, family life, opportunities for play and work has been denied to them. They have experienced and lived a life of social exclusion which clearly demonstrates violation of their rights as equal human beings. Children being a susceptible group stand a greater chance of discrimination and they are least able to assert their rights enshrined in the international conventions. Before beginning the discourse on children's rights, the chapter would explicate the evolution of the concept of childhood.

Conception of Childhood

Societies develop the ideological framework about the age categories or life cycle phases, thus making childhood a social construct. The origin of the concept of childhood has been a matter of debate. As pointed by Philippe Aries (1962) that 'in medieval society the idea of childhood did not exist'. According to him it was not until the mid-eighteenth century that child was given a central place in the family. The evidence for his thesis was derived from the visual arts, literary texts and manuals, styles of dress, references to the child as 'it', and the use of the names of dead children for later births in the same family. Though his methodology and findings have been heavily criticized by numerous writers, he remains a significant contributor to the historiography of childhood. He owns the credit of drawing attention to the possibility of a developmental notion of childhood. As to whether the idea of childhood existed in the medieval period, the current consensus is that although prior to the seventeenth century children were viewed differently from today, there nevertheless existed a perception of their distinctiveness.

Indian conceptions of childhood have been very different from the western world. In ancient Indian law, Laws of Manu, the child had been located at the bottom of the social pyramid. The apex position was reserved for the householder, an adult male. The lower social status of the child was also evident in Manu's mourning prescriptions in case of child's death. The younger the deceased the shorter was the mourning period and the less elaborate are the funeral rites. Children along with women, aged, sick and infirm deserved societal protection (Kakar 1979:8-9). In classical Sanskrit literature, children rarely figure as individuals in their own right, with activities, reactions and feelings separate from those of their all powerful parents (ibid:18). Though these historical conceptions have changed to a large extent by the changes in the family structures, parental beliefs and attitudes, the children have been assigned a social status associated with minimal decision-making prerogatives. The decisions are routinely made for and about children irrespective of the impact of these judgements on the welfare of children. According to Calkins, Lukenbill and Mateer (1979:90), "Children are often regarded more as things subject to the control and convenience of others, rather than as persons with wants and interests of their own". Thus, the rights of children have been limited by considerations about their inherent vulnerability and central to this are concerns about their capacity to manage political and civil participatory rights.

The Ideological Shift

There has been a shift in attitude towards children's rights in the past decade. Whereas previously the approach was welfare-oriented and sought only to provide for children's basic welfare needs, in recent years children have also come to be viewed as holders of a wider range of rights. International law provides some guidance to the member countries for law and policy making in this jurisdiction. It has been a tough proposition for children in India, as the country represents a huge proportion of the world's child population posing enormous challenges for the Government to meet the needs and protect the rights of the children under its jurisdiction. The task is further complicated by the high rate of population growth which makes it difficult to sustain the necessary resources. In a diverse and multicultural society compounded with conditions like poverty, illiteracy, child abuse, and child labour, the efforts to combat discrimination and societal attitudes needs to be continuous and sustained. There have been certain positive attempts by the Government towards tackling the grim situation; however, the scope of such initiatives still remains narrow.

The National Policy for Children (1974) in India defined children as its "supremely important asset", thereby resting massive responsibility on the Government to protect and nurture the posterity in the best possible way. Children as such are a vulnerable group and any kind of difficult circumstances render them even more vulnerable. Hence, they become easy victims of abuse or neglect which hampers their overall development. Children with disability are doubly jeopardized in our country's context. Thus, this vulnerable group deserves special protection and safeguards for equally dignified existence in the society. Though the issues related to child rights are gaining ground in India, the children with disabilities largely remain segregated in this sphere as well.

The Convention on the Rights of the Child remains a landmark document which comprehensively covers civil and political, social, economic and cultural rights of children. The issues concerning rights of children with disabilities are complex because of several interacting factors. The social and cultural milieu of India does not grant complete freedom to the child in terms of making decisions for himself/herself. Children have been considered a prime responsibility and possession of the parents and their families. The result has been a complete control of the children's actions and thought processes by the parents or guardians. The thought underlying this control which is sometimes coercive leads to unrealized potentials of the children.

Children and young people, as human beings, are entitled to the full range of human rights protections. These rights are primarily laid down in the UN Convention on the Rights of the Child (CRC), 1989 and the UN Convention on the Rights of the Persons with Disabilities, 2006. The present chapter examines the relevance of these international covenants and the obligations placed on government with respect to protection of rights of children with disabilities in India. The child welfare practices have become rights oriented only during the twentieth century, prior to this children were recipients of welfare measures (Bajpai 2003). It would thus be interesting to elucidate how these changes were brought about and CRC was formulated which is considered to be a landmark international child's rights legislation.

Evolution of the Rights Perspective

The development of human rights could be divided into three stages; first stage was in philosophical works, second stage was the transition from theory to practice and the third stage was the official international Declarations commencing from the Universal Declaration of Human Rights in 1948 (Cheria *et al.,* 2004). Human rights have evolved from the concept of natural rights. The earliest direct precursor to human rights might be found in the notions of 'natural right' developed by classical Greek philosophers, such as Aristotle, but this concept was more fully developed by Thomas Aquinas in his Summa Theologica. For several centuries Aquinas' conception held sway: there were goods or behaviours that were naturally right because God ordained it so. What was naturally right could be ascertained by humans by 'right reason' - thinking properly (Heard, 1997).The first philosopher who fully made natural rights the source of his moral and political philosophy and detached if from divine authority was Thomas Hobbes through his book titled, *Leviathan* published in 1651. Hobbes argued that it is human nature to love one's self best and seek one's own good. Since it is unavoidable for human beings to follow their nature, it becomes a right to do so. According to Hobbes, to deny this right is to deny that we have a right to be human. However, the divine basis of natural right was still pursued for more than a century after Hobbes published his *Leviathan*. John Locke wrote a strong defence of natural rights in the late 17th century with the publication of his *Two Treatises on Government,* but his arguments were filled with references to what God had ordained or given to mankind (ibid). Another philosopher who contributed extensively to the theory oh human rights was Jean-Jacques Rousseau. Through his *Social Contract* he not only lambasted attempts to tie religion to the foundations of political order but disentangled the rights of a society from natural rights. In

Rousseau's view, the rights in a civil society are sacred: "But the social order is a sacred right which serves as a basis for other rights. And as it is not a natural right, it must be one founded on covenants" (Rousseau, 1968). The prominent thought systems of social scientists advocating similar ideas had a great impact on the development of international convenants on human rights.

The second stage in the history of human rights is the transition from theory to practice. In the late 1700s two revolutions occurred which drew heavily on this concept. In 1776 most of the British colonies in North America proclaimed their independence from the British Empire in a document which still stirs feelings, and debate, the U.S. Declaration of Independence. In 1789 the people of France overthrew their monarchy and established the first French Republic. Out of the revolution came the "Declaration of the Rights of Man." The term natural rights eventually fell into disfavour, but the concept of universal rights took root.

The third stage commenced with the Universal Declaration of Human Rights, 1948 after the Second World War in which the assertion of human rights was both universal and positive. This preceded a range of international Conventions, Covenants, Declarations and other treaties from the United Nations that have followed the tradition.

The general rule is that children are accorded the same basic rights as adults. However, because of their physical and mental immaturity, children are especially vulnerable and require special rights to protect them and to meet their unique needs. It is because of this immaturity that children must postpone the exercise of some civil rights until they become adults - so increasing the obligation on adults to ensure that the rights of the child are defended (Castelle, 1990). The children's rights movement is a historical and modern movement committed to the acknowledgement, expansion, and/or regression of the rights of children around the world. Thomas Spence's *The Rights of Infants* (1796) was an early assertion of the natural rights of children.

In USA, the children's rights were first acknowledged in the 1800s with the orphan train. The name 'orphan train' originated with the railroad trains that transported the street and orphan children to their new adoptive homes or workplace. In the big cities, when a child's parents died, the child frequently had to go to work to support himself or herself. Boys generally became factory or coal workers, and girls became prostitutes or saloon girls, or else went to work in small shops, which paid only starvation wages. By the late 1800s, the orphan train had stopped running altogether, but its principles lived on. In the early twentieth century, moves began to promote the idea of children's rights as distinct from those of adults and as requiring explicit recognition. The Polish educationalist Janusz Korczak wrote of the rights of children in his book, *How to Love a Child* (1919); a later book was entitled, *The Child's Right to Respect* (1929). In 1917, following the Russian Revolution, the Moscow branch of the organization, Proletkult produced a Declaration of Children's Rights. However, the first effective attempt to promote children's rights was the Declaration of the Rights of the Child, drafted by Eglantyne Jebb in 1923 and adopted by the League of Nations in 1924. This was accepted by the United Nations on its formation and updated in 1959, and replaced with a more extensive UN Convention on the Rights of the Child in 1989. The formulation of the CRC has had a tremendous impact on the child's right movement throughout the world.

The ratification of the CRC has placed an obligation on the member states to uphold and protect child rights. India ratified the convention in December 1992 and committed itself to promotion and protection of the rights enshrined in the convention for its 380 million children below the age of fourteen years (GOI, 1999), 157,863,145 children in the age group of 0-6 years (Census of India 2001) and thirty-five million children with disabilities(Bajpai 2003:1). India has responded to the rights and participation of its population with disabilities through the legislation called the Persons with Disabilities Act enacted in 1995. It would be imperative to present an overview of this legislation before analyzing the CRC's implications in the Indian context.

The Persons with Equal Opportunities, Protection of Rights and Full Participation Act, 1995: An Overview

The Act was enacted in 1995 "to give effect to the Proclamation on the Full Participation and Equality of People with Disabilities in the Asian and Pacific Region". There are altogether fourteen chapters and seventy-three sections in the Act. The legislation aimed for the following provisions as adopted by the Economic and Social Commission for Asian and Pacific Region:

(i) to spell out the responsibility of the State towards the prevention of disabilities, protection of rights, provision of medical care, education, training, employment and rehabilitation of persons with disabilities;

(ii) to create a barrier free environment for persons with disabilities.

(iii) to remove any discrimination against persons with disabilities in the sharing of development benefits, *vis-à-vis* non-disabled persons.

(iv) to counteract any situation of the abuse and exploitation of persons with disabilities;

(v) to lay down a strategy for comprehensive development of programmes and services and equalization of opportunities for persons with disabilities;

(vi) to make special provision of the integration of the persons with disabilities in the social mainstream.

The salient features of the Act include :

- Defining the seven categories of disability in Chapter I. According to the Act "disability" means blindness, low vision, leprosy cured, hearing impairment, locomotor disability, mental retardation and mental illness.
- Chapters II and III lay down the formation and functioning of the Central Coordination Committees and Executive Committees at the Centre and State levels respectively.
- Chapter IV directs the appropriate governments and local authorities to take certain steps for the prevention and occurrence of disabilities.
- Chapter V pertains to education. Every child with disability is entitled to a free education up to the age of 18 years. The government and local authorities must endeavour to promote integration of students with disabilities in normal schools, promote setting up of special schools in order to make them accessible to children living in any part of the country.
- The focus of Chapter VI is employment. It mandates identification of posts which could be reserved for the persons with disability and 3 per cent reservation of posts in the government establishments.
- Chapter VII proclaims affirmative action in terms of making schemes for providing aids and appliances to persons with disabilities and preferential allotment of land for purpose of setting up business, special recreation centres, special schools, research centres and factories by entrepreneurs with disabilities.
- Chapter VIII specifically deals with non discrimination of person with disabilities in transport, on roads, built environment in terms of increasing accessibility to things or places. It also lays down that a government

employee could not be discriminated against his able-bodied colleagues on the basis of his/her disability.

- Chapter IX directs to promote and sponsor research in disability prevention and other disability issues.
- Chapter X lays down rules for recognition of institutions for persons with disabilities.
- Chapter XI asserts establishment and maintenance of institution for persons with severe (80% or more) disabilities. It is, however, not mandatory for the government. It also clearly states that every other institution established under sub-section 1 of this chapter should be maintained as per the government prescribed rules.
- Chapter XII calls for an appointment of Chief Commissioner for persons with disability by the Central Government. The functions of the Chief Commissioner include: coordinate the work of the Commissioners appointed by the State Government as per Section 60 of the Act, monitor the utilization of the funds disbursed by the Central Government, take steps to safeguard the rights and facilities made available to persons with disabilities, and submitting reports to the Central Government on the implementation of the Act at such intervals as the government may prescribe.
- Chapter XIII instructs the appropriate government and local authorities within the limits of their economic capacity and development to undertake the cause of rehabilitation of the persons with disabilities.

These provisions of the Act would be useful when the CRCs guidelines and stipulations would be contextualized to India. Nonetheless, it is important to mention that despite of promulgation of the Act a decade ago most of its directions are unrealized.

Convention on the Rights of the Child: An Overview

The Convention of the Rights of the Child (CRC) is a successor of the Declaration of the Rights, adopted by the League of the Nations in 1924 and the UN Declaration of Rights of the Child of 1959. Its success could be attributed to the wide range of rights; social, cultural, economic, civil and political that it covers. Though it is difficult for an international document to be all pervasive that is catering to all children differing culturally, socially and economically, the convention encompasses a wide range of rights pertaining to all children, certain sections are dedicated to special categories of children or children under different circumstances.

The Convention on the Rights of the Child (CRC) is an instrument that upholds and protects the rights of the children and adolescents taking due consideration of their survival, development, protection and participation needs. The first article of the CRC spells out the age criterion for consideration. It states that every human being below the age of 18 would be regarded as the child unless the law applicable to the child in a member state spells out another age criterion.

Some of the general principles of the CRC which are applicable to all children are primarily the children must not suffer any kind of discrimination based on the "child's or his or her parent's or legal guardian's race, colour, sex, language, religion, political or other opinion, national, ethnic or social origin, property, disability, birth or other status." (Articles 2), secondly all children have a right to survival and development in all aspects of their lives, including the physical, emotional, psychosocial, cognitive, social and cultural. (Articles 6 and 27), thirdly, the best interests of the child must be a primary consideration in all decisions or actions that affect the child or children as a group. This holds true whether decisions are made by governmental, administrative or judicial authorities, or by families themselves (Article 3). According to UN (2006), the principle that the best interests of the child are a primary consideration in all actions concerning children is supreme. By virtue of their relative immaturity, young children are reliant on responsible authorities to assess and represent their rights and best interests in relation to decisions and actions that affect their well-being, while taking account of their views and evolving capacities. The principle of best interests appears repeatedly within the Convention (including in Articles 9, 18, 20 and 21, which are most relevant to early childhood). The principle of best interests applies to all actions concerning children and requires active measures to protect their rights and promote their survival, growth, and well-being, as well as measures to support and assist parents and others who have day-to-day responsibility for realizing children's rights. Finally the children have the right to peaceful assembly, to be active participants in all matters affecting their lives, to express their opinions freely and to have their views heard and taken seriously (Article 15).

Other notable features of the CRC which make it distinct, comprehensive and complete document on child rights are :

- The Convention on the Rights of the Child contains civil and political, and social, economic and cultural rights in a single document. The right to a name and to a nationality (Article 7) and the right to freedom of thought, conscience and religion (Article 14) are both examples of civil and political rights. The social, economic and cultural rights contained in the Convention include, amongst many others, the right to education (Article 28), the right to health and health services (Article 24), and the right to an adequate standard of living (Article 27). These provisions make the document very comprehensive and diverse.

- Broadly the civil, political, economic and cultural rights of every child could be clustered around four classes- (Bajpai 2003:18) :
  1. *The Right to Survival:* This includes the right to life, the highest attainable standard of health and nutrition, and adequate standard of living.
  2. *The Right to Protection:* This includes freedom from all forms of exploitation, abuse, inhuman or degrading treatment, and neglect, including the right to special protection in situations of emergency and armed conflicts.
  3. *The Right to Development:* This includes the right to education, support for early childhood development and care, social security, and the right to leisure, recreation and cultural activities.
  4. *The Right to Participation:* This includes respect for the views of the child, freedom of expression, access to appropriate information, and freedom of thought, conscience and religion.
- Other thematic clusters proposed by the UN Committee on the Rights of the Child are :
  1. Civil Rights and freedoms considers amongst other rights, a child's right to an identity, freedom of conscience and freedom of association.
  2. The articles on Family Environment and Alternative Care consider the role of the family in the care of the child, and the part the state plays. They also relate to what must happen if a child is deprived of his or her family, for example the special measures of protection afforded to children in institutional care.
  3. Some articles address the health of children and the health services that are provided, and the measures of protection a state should take to assure an adequate standard of living for a child

and could be clubbed under Basic Health and Welfare.

4. Education and Cultural activities: These articles include standards related not only the educational facilities that are available, but also the quality of the education that is provided and how this prepares the child for a meaningful life in society. The child's need for recreation is addressed as well.
5. Special Protection Measures: This cluster of articles considers the needs of groups of children who are at particular risk and who may require special protection. This includes refugee children and those in conflicts, children who are exploited through labour, or through sexual exploitation, and children who are subjected to violence. It also refers to children who are in conflict with the law, and the misuse of substances by children and adolescents.

The CRC has emerged as a useful tool for encouraging states to take steps to improve the conditions in which their children and adolescents live as it has attempted to group together civil, political, social, economic and cultural rights, laid out clear recommendations for action and managed a wide ratification from countries all over the world. The CRC stipulations have got a double sanction with the promulgation of UN Convention on the Persons with Disabilities which has an exclusive section (Article 7) on children with disabilities. The article strictly directs for protection of rights of children with disabilities at par with other children. It further ordains all actions concerning children with disabilities must consider the "best interests", they must express their voices and concerns in all matters affecting them, and they must be provided with disability and age appropriate assistance for realising their rights.

The above discussion has helped in getting an overall picture of the provisions of the CRC and would further help in developing an understanding its relevance and application for the children with disabilities.

Children with Disabilities and the CRC

The children with disabilities are identified by their impairment rather than children first who happen to have an impairment. Consequently, they are viewed solely in terms of their medical needs out of context of their social and educational needs and rights. "Disabled children in virtually all societies suffer discrimination, violence and abuse, poverty, exclusion and institutionalisation" (International Save the Children Alliance 2001:2) despite the lengthy provisions of the CRC and its wide ratifications by the member nations. Jones (2000) after an exploration of recent Country Reports to the UN Committee on the Rights of the Child reported that, in most cases, disabled children are mentioned under Article 23 only, with the focus on rehabilitation and 'special care.' Occasionally disabled children are referred to under Article 28 (the right to education); very rarely under other Articles. It is rare to find more than a passing reference to disabled children in the government literature on child rights issues.

There are approximately 2 billion children in the world, of whom, it is conservatively estimated, as many as 100 million have disabilities. There are hundreds of thousands of children with disabilities who are condemned to live their lives in institutions, often deprived not only of love and affection, but also of the most basic physical care and intellectual stimulation. Armed conflicts and political violence, which have such devastating impacts on children's lives, also contribute heavily to the toll of disability: they are now the leading causes of injury, impairment and physical disability in children, and only 3 per cent of children disabled as a result of war receive any rehabilitative care (UN, 1997).

The CRC is the most widely ratified document of the world and with intent applies to all children without an exception. This however remains a cherished dream for the member nations as the vulnerable children are often deprived of their basic rights. Children with disabilities are one such disadvantaged group and also the focus of this chapter. There is little doubt over the efficacy of the CRC for safeguarding the rights of the children with disabilities but the relaxed attitude of the ratifying nations towards its implementation has been a matter of grave concern. The member nations lack the adequate machinery to implement what either exists or has been designed keeping pace with the rights perspective.

Apart from the general application of all the sections to the children with disabilities, the Article 23 has been distinctly defined for them. There would be an attempt to look at the some specific articles and few clusters of articles to examine their relevance and extent of observance in context of India.

The opening article lays emphasis on the age of the child and defines a limiting criterion of 18 years unless in the law applicable to the child, majority is attained earlier. The Census of India defines persons below the age of fourteen years as children. Most of the Government programmes on children are targeted for the age group below fourteen years (Bajpai, 2003:2). The newer policies and laws, however, are subscribing to the new age criterion laid down by the CRC like the Juvenile Justice Act, 2000 and the National Policy for the Persons with Disabilities, 2006. There is a need of greater uniformity of the age criterion defined for children.

The second article ensures that every child's rights are secured irrespective of child's or his parents' race, colour, sex, language, religion, political or other opinion, national, ethnic or social origin, property, disability, birth or other status. The Convention overtly mentions through this article that the child should not be discriminated against and his/her rights need to be safeguarded irrespective of his physical, social, cultural or economical status, there are however reported violations of rights of children with disabilities.

The convention would be reviewed in the four clusters containing rights to survival, protection, development and participation. Since the focus of the chapter is children with disabilities, it may be vital to discuss the articles which specifically relate to their rights. The given articles appear to cast a greater impact on the rights of the children with disabilities; this however does not indicate that the other articles are irrelevant to them. It is reiterated here that children with disabilities must not be seen as a different category of children having a different experience of childhood. The rest of the articles also are equally applicable to them, what is highlighted in this chapter only designates greater importance with reference to children having special needs.

Right to Survival

The survival rights include the right to life and the right to the highest standard of health and medical care attainable (Storer, 1994). The right to survival is thus indicated within Articles 6, 9, 10, 22, 23, 24, 26, 27 and 30 of the Convention.

Article 6 has great implications on children to be born with disabilities. As per the article every child has the "inherent right to life" and state parties have to "ensure to the maximum extent possible the survival and development of the child". The newer techniques of prenatal screening and amniocentesis detect the foetal abnormality at a stage when medical termination is possible and most often than not it is carried out if the baby to be born was not found to be "healthy", "perfect" and "normal". The attitude has an inherent desire for children which are so called normal and healthy by the parents and the intervening medical practitioners. The other side of the story of denying "right to life" to a child with disability is often suppressed. The fact however has been well illustrated by Alison Davis (1999) in his article where he argued that every human life - to be of infinite value immaterial of the fact that it has abilities other than as defined as normal. This provision is safely ignored for children who are detected for a disability at the prenatal stage. This unrighteous behaviour upholds the medical supremacy over the natural diversity. The disabled children are regarded as abnormal and unwanted and through advancements in medical field, they are quietly aborted. India gave a legal sanction to such medical terminations of pregnancy through its Medical Termination of Pregnancy Act, 1971. The section 2 of the Act states that a registered medical practitioner is entitled to perform an abortion if the length of the pregnancy exceeds twelve weeks but does not exceed twenty weeks, if not less than two registered medical practitioners, are of opinion found in good faith that there is substantial risk that if the child were born, it would suffer from such physical or mental abnormalities as to be seriously handicapped. This inadvertently perpetuates the "normal" definitions and cultures and gradual progression towards a medically created superior generation.

Article 23 of the Convention explicitly spells out the right of children with disabilities but their rights are in no way confined to Article 23; rather, the provisions of that article were intended to ensure that the disabled child had maximum opportunity to fulfil all the rights set out in the Convention. The first out of the four sub-sections of the article recognises that a physically or mentally challenged child should enjoy "a full and decent life in conditions which ensure dignity promote self reliance and facilitate child's active participation in the community". This segment underlines the fact that disability in a child must not result in complete dependence and overprotection by the families. More often than not the children with disabilities are seen incapable of living their lives fully and are looked at with pity and compassion. Their participation in the activities of the community like other children is restrained thus invoking in them the ideas of self pity and incapability. If they are reared otherwise that is, in an environment promoting independence and self-reliance they are sure to have the confidence to develop their abilities for realising their potentials.

The second sub-section of the same article asserts that children with disabilities have the right to "special care", and maintains that this shall be offered by the State. The available resources are to be made accessible to the eligible child or his parents/guardians keeping in mind the child's requirements and familial circumstances. Though the sub-section offers supplementary support to the child and its families to help him/her realise its potentials, its translation into reality is subject to availability of resources and assessing the child's and familial circumstances. The third sub-section is an extension of the previous one where such services and supports must be provided free of cost to the family which has poor financial status. The aim is to provide access to "education, training, health care services, rehabilitation services, preparation for employment and recreation opportunities in a manner conducive to the child's achieving the fullest possible *social integration* and *individual development,* including his cultural and spiritual development" [emphasis added]. It is acknowledged that it is extremely important for the child to achieve social integration and individual development for which equal opportunities for education, health, rehabilitation, employment and recreation. Disabled children throughout history have suffered segregation in all spheres of life. It is the most vital and most difficult objective of the convention as the removal of social, physical and attitudinal barriers erected by the society for the children with disabilities. This has turned out to be a complex proposition for the member nations.

The fourth sub-section of the article highlights exchange of information in the field of "preventive health care and of medical, psychological and functional treatment of disabled children including dissemination of and access to information concerning methods of rehabilitation, education and vocational services" within countries of the world so as to have a wider experience and exposure of the issues and concerns and improvement of skills and capabilities for providing better infrastructural and social support to the children with disabilities.

The ratification of international covenants calls for commitment and action at three levels: legislative, financial and ideological. Whenever an act or policy is enacted following ratification of a convention, its implementation depends on the financial and ideological commitment the nation's government shows towards change. The Indian government has developed four national level institutes for specific disabilities. However, the prime objective of these institutes is rehabilitation. Though the government relies heavily on the voluntary sector for provision of basic facilities, it has allocated only 30 per cent of the planned expenditure on the voluntary sector and the rest is reserved for the national institutes and factories it has set for aids and appliances (Alur, 2002) for meeting their rehabilitation objectives, which are mostly health and welfare oriented. The education of children with disabilities is the prerogative of the special schools and the ordinary schools have not been able to cater to the diverse needs of the children with disabilities. India is still under the grip of prejudice and sympathy for the children with disabilities and do not consider them as part of the normal populace having differential abilities. This has largely hampered the aim of achieving social integration of children with disabilities and has led to their invisibility and isolation.

Article 24 of the CRC says that a child has the right to the highest standard of health and medical care attainable.

States shall place special emphasis on the provision of primary and preventive health care, public health education and the reduction of infant mortality. They shall encourage international co-operation in this regard and strive to see that no child is deprived of access to effective health services. In the light of Article 24 of the Convention, the member nations are supposed to focus and place on priority on the main health issues by establishing national programmes and allocating resources.

Needless to say the children with disabilities have complex health needs and there is a possibility of them requiring health services throughout the life span. They may require medical and nursing support from health care providers and school health teams, therapy services including physiotherapy, occupational therapy, speech therapy and advice about diet, aids and appliances and their parents might require guidance on child development. As per the National Policy for Persons with Disabilities (2006) currently, these services are largely available in and around urban areas. The policy lays down that the services run by professionals will be extended to cover uncovered and un-served areas as seventy-five per cent persons with disabilities live in rural areas. Further, privately owned rehabilitation service centres shall be regulated for maintenance of minimum standards which would be laid down. The policy is rich in its content and promises but what remains to be seen is its implementation. It is imperative that these policy documents are translated into reality for ensuring the survival and development rights to the children with disabilities.

Right to Development

The development rights include provisions for education - both formal and informal and the right to a standard of living which is adequate for the child's physical, mental, spiritual, moral and social development (Storer, 1994). The development of the child would also depend on the access to information, play and leisure, cultural activities and the right to freedom of thought, conscience and religion. These provisions are illustrated in Articles 14, 28, 29 and 31.

The role of education in child's development is a crucial one. Article 28 of the Convention lays down that every child has a right to education, and the State's duty is to ensure that primary education is free and compulsory, to encourage different forms of secondary education accessible to every child and to make higher education available to all on the basis of capacity. Article 29 puts forward the aims of education. Education shall aim at developing the child's personality, talents and mental and physical abilities to the fullest extent. Education shall prepare the child for an active adult life in a free society and foster respect for the child's parents, his or her own cultural identity, language and values, and for the cultural background and values of others.

There are constitutional and policy statements on universalisation of primary education in India but the goal remains unrealized till date. Though the growth in the education sector has been phenomenal after the Independence, education for the disabled has not received adequate impetus. The NSSO (National Sample Survey Organization) Survey of 2002 estimated 18.49 million people with disability in India. There have been reported discrepancies regarding estimating the number of children with disabilities in India. Singal (2006) has cited Office of the Chief Commissioner for Persons with Disabilities (2003), which notes that the figures available are highly unreliable and, depending on how conservative the estimate is made, there are between 6 million and 30 million children with disabilities in India. It further notes that the "Rehabilitation Council of India takes the figure of 30 million disabled children as the best estimate". These variations highlight the lack of availability of reliable estimates of children with disabilities for whom provisions need to be made. Thus, the task of responding to their needs is made even more difficult. Such discrepancies in numbers are also evident in the educational status of children with disabilities.

Mukhopadhyay and Mani (2002) state that there is "inconsistency in data (regarding the enrolment levels of children with disabilities) from various sources" (p. 103). They note that according to a National Council of Education survey carried out in 1998, about 84,000 children with disabilities are enrolled in schools. They also quote unpublished data gathered for the Ministry of Human Resource Development in 1999, which suggests that approximately 55,000 children with disabilities are enrolled in schools. Mukhopadhyay and Mani contrast these figures with the total population of children with disabilities in the 5 to 15 years age group, estimated to be about 10.39 million. Hence they state that "the picture (of school enrolment for children with disabilities) is dismal" (Mukhopadhyay and Mani, 2002, p. 101). The figures given by Mukhopadhyay and Mani suggest that less than 1 per cent of children with disabilities attend school. A position paper drafted by the National Council for Educational Research and Training (2005) notes that, "the Office of the Chief Commissioner of Persons with Disabilities stated that not more than 4 per cent of children with disabilities have access to education" (cited in Singal, 2006). These statistics may present a dismal picture but it is important to add that some efforts had been initiated in the field of Education for the children with disabilities. The scheme of Integrated Education for Disabled children was launched in 1974 and its implementation was entrusted to the Department of Education in 1982.

The National Policy on Education, 1986 brought the education of this group of children under Equal Education Opportunity Provision. The Persons with Disabilities Act, 1995 requires the Government to provide free education in an appropriate environment till the age of 18 years. The Act also promotes the integration of disabled children into normal schools. As per the Act, the Government should formulate schemes to provide part-time classes, non-formal education and education through open schools and universities for children with special needs. The Act envisages a comprehensive scheme with transport facilities, free books, uniforms and other materials, schools without architectural barriers, which provide a restructured curriculum, a modified examination system as well as scholarships for the benefit of these children. However, exclusionary policies and practices that deny admission to disabled children are widely prevalent all over the country.

The non-statutory initiatives particularly by the NGO sector have been worth appreciating, there are number of NGOs working in the field of disability. Even the government sector has recognized the need to collaborate and support the NGO Initiatives in the field of health, education and rehabilitation programmes for the disabled in India. Though the contribution of the NGOs in the disability sector is valuable, it is not widespread. They work under limitation of funds and support from the Government and various International and National funding organisations.

Other development essentials as stated in Article 31 are leisure, recreation and cultural activities to which every child has a right. The children with disabilities are deprived of these normal experiences as other children because of the inaccessibility of the public places and segregated educational experiences. According to Abidi (2007), the disabled people are invisible at public places like markets, cinema halls or parks, colleges and universities because the physical environment and the transportation system are not only unfriendly but hostile. It is thus difficult for the disabled people to venture out compromising on their safety and dignity. Easy, accessible and economical public transportation is the key of any person's freedom of movement especially for people with disabilities. He adds in the news feature that even a decade after the passage of the PWD Act, India's capital does not run disability friendly buses which leads to segregation and invisibility of the disabled population.

Behind the instances lay attitudes which viewed the life of a disabled child as being of less worth, less importance and less potential than that of an able-bodied child. Those attitudes must be challenged as the overall development of a child with a disability is as important as his/her normally developing peer. This requires political action at every level, including legal reform to end all forms of discrimination, public education programmes, practical action to support families and communities in challenging prejudice and social exclusion, campaigns to raise awareness of the human rights of children with disabilities, programmes to end institutionalization of children, and positive images of children with disabilities in the media.

Right to Protection

The protection of the rights of the child include protection from discrimination for children without families, freedom from all forms of exploitation, inhuman abuse or degrading treatment and neglect and the right to special protection in situations of emergency and armed conflict (Storer, 1994; UNICEF, 1996).

The Articles underscoring the child's protection are 2, 7, 16, 19, 20, 32, 33, 34, 35 and 36. For the disabled child, the principle of non-discrimination outlined in Article 2 underlies all Articles of the CRC. Direct discrimination is the most obvious, where a disabled child is treated in an inferior way to non-disabled children. For instance, it is most likely in India for a disabled child to be denied admission in an ordinary school on the basis on his/her disability. Indirect discrimination is more subtle, but equally damaging. For example, The PWD Act and the education policy may state that mainstream schools are open to all children, but in reality, disabled children are still not be able to attend school because nothing has been done to make education more accessible: the curriculum is still as rigid, buildings have too many steps, teachers lack skills and awareness, etc.

The Articles 32, 33, 34, 35 and 36 call for action by the state parties against any forms of exploitation and abuse of children. It has been noted that children who live with a physical, sensory, intellectual or mental health disability are among the most stigmatized and marginalized of all the world's children. While all children are at risk of being victims of violence, disabled children find themselves at significantly increased risk because of stigma, negative traditional beliefs and ignorance. Lack of social support, limited opportunities for education, employment or participation in the community further isolates disabled children and their families, leading to increased levels of stress and hardship. Children with disabilities are also often targeted by abusers, who see them as easy victims (UNICEF 2005). There is a likelihood of abuse and violence in homes, educational and custodial settings, and institutions, children's homes within the criminal justice system, community and workplace and any physical or mental impairments add to the vulnerability of the child. The fact has been substantiated by Bajpai (2003: 210) where she mentions that children with disabilities with problems of communication and comprehension are particularly vulnerable to sexual abuse. Thus children with disabilities must be included in all violence intervention efforts intended for the general population of children. While the role of international organizations and government agencies is crucial in addressing the epidemic of violence and abuse against children with disabilities, this cannot be done without a significant leadership role also being taken by organizations, community leaders and members of civil society.

Civil society must work with families of disabled children and disability advocacy groups to take a leading role in advocating change to ensure inclusion of individuals with disability throughout society. Through mass media campaigns, collaboration with government officials at all levels, advocacy for progressive legislation and funding that increases the inclusion of disabled children in schools and communities, civil society has the ability to shape and redefine better and more inclusive attitudes towards disabled children - thus lessening the likelihood that they will become victims of violence or abuse (UNICEF 2005).

Right to Participation

Participation is "the nature and extent of a person's involvement in life situations" (WHO, 1997). It includes the activities of personal maintenance, mobility, social relationships, education, leisure, spirituality, and community life.

Articles 12 and 13 of the CRC highlight the importance of the child's participation in matters concerning him and his/her opinion must be given due weight in accordance to his age and maturity and also possess the right to expression along with freedom to seek, receive and impart information and ideas of all kinds.

The researchers and scholars have established that children with disabilities tend to be more restricted in their participation in daily activities (e.g., active recreation, household tasks, and social engagements) than their peers, and that the scope of their activities is limited (Brown & Gordon, 1987). Also the participation of children and youth with disabilities decreases as children grow up so that, by adulthood, their participation is severely restricted; typically, they take part in passive, often home-based, activities (Brown & Gordon, 1987; Crapps *et al.*, 1985; Dempsey, 1991; Pollock & Stewart, 1990) and finally that children with disabilities often feel socially isolated (Anderson & Clarke, 1982; Blum *et al.*, 1991; Cadman *et al.*, 1987; Law & Dunn, 1993).

Participation is a vital aspect of a child's socialization and a cornerstone of child protection, ensuring that the best interests of the child remain in focus, and is fundamental to the child's understanding of their role and responsibilities in the democratic process. It is therefore vital that parents, service providers, and policy makers concerned with children with disabilities understand the factors that promote or inhibit children's participation in order to provide a conducive environment for child's participation and development.

Conclusion

The chapter has examined the relevance and application of the CRC to children with disabilities in India. Children with disabilities are not benefitting from equal rights to others in India due to strongly entrenched stigma and discrimination, and are certainly not receiving any further help to assist with their disabilities. Until recently, disability and child policies have been paternalistic, based on charitable interventions as opposed to rights. Society has strong negative attitudes of children, especially disabled children, and made assumptions of their ability to express their views and participate in policy and planning.

It is important to take a holistic approach to disability. All the rights in the Convention must be considered in respect of disabled children, and disabled children should be considered when examining the implementation of all the rights in the Convention. The Convention provides a framework of principles for monitoring law, policy and practice in respect of disabled children. The Standard Rules on the Equalization of Opportunities for Persons with Disabilities (1993) and UN Convention on the Rights of

Persons with Disabilities (2006) provide a source of detailed guidance on what should be done and how to do it. Those two documents should be used by the Committee and others as complementary tools in promoting the rights of disabled children.

The action must be taken at every level - international, regional, national, local and community - to effectively promote the rights of disabled children. At the international level, the Committee had a clear role to play by rigorously scrutinizing States parties reports, highlighting the situation of disabled children, and promoting the application of the Standard Rules. Learning from exchange of experience, research, expertise and information, and good practice between countries must be fostered and encouraged.

The national government must take action to support the families of disabled children, promote access to education, train teachers to work in inclusive schools, enhance access to adequate health care, and provide practical help within villages and local communities. Such action would necessarily include legal reform and implementation, development of policies to promote opportunities for disabled children, reconsideration of budgets and reallocation of resources.

Like all other children, disabled children have the right to participate in the decisions that affect them but they are often denied this right. It is difficult for the adults to recognize the capacity and right of the child to express his opinion and participate in the decision making process and when the child suffers a disability then the adults have greater difficulties in accepting his/her competency. This fact is compounded by protectiveness on the part of carers which sought to shield the children from the responsibility of participation. It is therefore imperative to begin to explore ways of challenging the lack of belief in disabled children. There were many reasons for promoting more active participation in their own lives. First, decisions made about or on behalf of a child would be better informed and more likely to produce positive outcomes if the child himself or herself was involved in the process. The views, experiences and knowledge of the child must be an important part of any planning or decision-making. Second, the process of participation was a central part of learning to take responsibility, to make decisions, to develop self-esteem and confidence. It was hard for any child to learn those skills if no confidence is ever placed in him or her by adults; it was profoundly more difficult for a disabled child who faced prejudice and exclusion everyday of his or her life and who was constantly confronted by a self-image defined by society as negative and of little worth. It was therefore even more important that disabled children exercise their right to participate actively. Finally, by denying children the right to be heard we were denying them citizenship; they became non-people. Children whose voices were not heard or listened to were vulnerable to abuse, violence and exploitation by adults because they had no means of challenging their oppression.

There is an urgent need for advocacy within the rights context as the disabled children, more than any other group of children, are routinely denied the most basic rights. Bajpai (2003) embarks on advocacy and calls for it at different levels: child, parent, family, community and society. The process of advocacy - persuading, arguing, winning over, influencing opinion formers and policy makers could give a much needed boost to any programme initiative. This is especially required for a country like ours which has most of the legal documents and policies in terms with the international covenants but is far behind in their implementation. There is a need to develop strategies to ensure that the rights of disabled children were respected, both as individuals and as a group. Every child should have access to the necessary medical care and treatment, to education, to help with independent living, to aids and appliances if needed. It is also therefore needed to change the physical environment to promote the active inclusion of all disabled children in society and provide them with similar opportunities to which they are as much entitled as their normal peers.

References

Abidi, Javed (2007). The Invisible Minority. *Disability News and Information Service*, Volume 5 Issue 3.

Anderson, E. M., & Clarke, L. (Eds.). (1982). *Disability and adolescence*. New York: Methuen.

Aries, Philippe (1962). *Centuries of Childhood*. New York: Vintage Books

Bajpai, Asha (2003). *Child Rights in India: Law, Policy, and Practice*. New Delhi: Oxford University Press.

Blum, R. W., Resnick, M. D., Nelson, R., & St. Germaine, A. (1991). Family and peer issues among adolescents with spina bifida and cerebral palsy. *Pediatrics*, 88(22), 280-285.

Brown, M., & Gordon, W. (1987). Impact of impairment on activity patterns of children. *Archives of Physical Medicine and Rehabilitation*, 68, 828-832.

Cadman, D., Boyle, M., Szatmari, P., & Offord, D. R. (1987). Chronic illness, disability, and mental and social well-being: Findings of the Ontario Child Health Study. *Pediatrics*, 79, 805-813.

Castelle, Kay (1990). *In the Child's Best Interest: A primer on the UN Convention on the Rights of the Child*. Greenwich: Plan International.

Calkins, Carl F., Ronald W. Lukenbill and William J. Mateer (1973). Children's Rights: An Introductory Sociological Review. *Peabody Journal of Education*, Vol. 50, No. 2. (January, 1973), pp. 89-109.

Cheria, Anita, Sriprapha Petcharamesree and Edwin (2004). *A human rights approach to development*. Bangalore: Books for Change (A Unit for ActionAid Karnataka Projects).

Crapps, J., Langone, J., & Swaim, S. (1985). Quality and quantity of participation in community environments by mentally retarded adults. Mental Retardation, 20, 123-29.

Davis, Alison (1999). *A Disabled Person's Perspective on Pre-Natal Screening*. Retrieved on 11th February 2007 from http://www.leeds.ac.uk/disability-studies/archiveuk/Davis/A%20Disabled%20Person.pdf

Dempsey, I. (1991). Parental roles in the post-school adjustment of their sons and daughters with a disability. Australia and New Zealand : *Journal of Developmental Disabilities*, 17(3), 313-320.

Heard, Andrew (1997). *Human Rights: Chimeras in Sheep's Clothing?* Retrieved from http://www.sfu.ca/~aheard/intro.html on 20th February 2007.

Jones, Hazel (2000). Disabled Children's Rights and the UN Convention on the Rights of the Child. *Disability Studies Quarterly, Fall 2000*, Volume 20, No. 4

Law, M., & Dunn, W. (1993). Perspectives on understanding and changing the environments of children with disabilities. *Physical and Occupational Therapy in Pediatrics*, 13(3), 1-17.

NSSO Survey (2002). National Sample Survey Organisation Ministry of Statistics and Programme Implementation, Government of India December 2003

Pollock, N., & Stewart, D. (1990). A survey of activity patterns and vocational readiness of young adults with physical disabilities. *Canadian Journal of Rehabilitation*, 4(1), 17-26.

Rousseau, Jean-Jacques (1968). *The Social Contract.* Baltimore : Penguin p. 50.

Singal, Nidhi (2006). Inclusive Education in India: International Concept, National Interpretation. *International Journal of Disability, Development and Education*, Vol. 53, No. 3, September 2006, pp. 351-369

Storer, G. (Ed.) (1994). *Promoting the Rights of the Child: A Training Package on the Rights of the Child for ISCA members and partners*, Bangalore: International Save the Children Alliance (Asia).

The Medical Termination of Pregnancy Act (1971). New Delhi: GOI

The Persons with Disabilities (Equal Opportunities, Protection of Rights and Full Participation) Act (1995). New Delhi: GOI.

UN (1997) CRC/C/66, Annex V, 16th Session, 6 October 1997. Retrieved from http://www.unhchr.ch/html/menu2/6/crc/doc/days/disabled.pdf on 2nd February 2007.

UN (2006). CRC/C/GC/7/Rev.1 20 September 2006. Retrieved from http://www.ohchr.org/english/bodies/crc/docs/AdvanceVersions/GeneralComment7Rev1.pdf on 14th February 2007

United Nations (2006). UN Convention on the Persons with Disabilities. Retrieved on 3rd January 2007 from http://www.un.org/esa/socdev/enable/rights/convtexte.htm

UNICEF (1989), U.N. Convention on the Rights of the Child, New York: UNICEF.

UNICEF (1996). The State of the World's Children 1995, New Delhi.

UNICEF(2005). UN Secretary Generals Report on Violence against Children Thematic Group on Violence against Disabled Children.Convened by at the United Nations, New York, July 28, 2005 Retrieved from http://www.violencestudy.org/IMG/doc/UNICEF_Violence_Againt_Disabled_Children_Report_-_Submitted_Version.doc on 23rd December 2006

World Health Organization. (1997). *International classification of impairments, activities and participation*: ICIDH-2 Beta Draft. Geneva: World Health Organization.

4

INCLUSIVE EDUCATION

In all the societies of the world there are still obstacles preventing persons with disabilities from exercising their rights and freedoms and making it difficult for them to participate fully in the activities of their societies. It is the responsibility of the States to take appropriate action to remove such obstacles. (UN Standard Rules, 1993)

Introduction

Children with disabilities are one of the most disadvantaged groups in our society. In addition to their perceptible physical and circumstantial limitations they are subjected to innumerable ways of social discrimination, impoverished education and reduced work opportunities. Disabled individuals are undeniably the victims of inequity, marginalization and of a vicious cycle of multiple deprivation. At every stage of life they face barriers either created architecturally or attitudinally by the society, which prevent them from leading a normal and productive life. Their situation is the silent tragedy of modern competitive world where they are prevented from participating in the normal activities of our society because of their physical or/and mental limitations.

It is unfortunate that the society in very subtle ways disables the person by labelling and exclusion. Philosophically there is a movement towards a more inclusive society that does not separate and segregate individuals based on the differences that are often misunderstood. Inclusion is a philosophy built on the belief that all people are equal and should be respected and valued, as an issue of basic human rights. It is an "unending set of processes" in which children and adults with disabilities have the opportunity to participate fully in all community activities offered to people who do not have disabilities (UNESCO, 1997).

Inclusive education could be regarded as an indispensable component of inclusion as schooling is a very important phase of all children's life. It is important that all children are given equal opportunities to develop their abilities and innate potentials. Presently the regular schools are unable to cater to the children with disabilities because of their unpreparedness towards them. The onus of coping in a regular school lies only with the disabled child and his/her parents. In case of failure, the teachers blame the parents and warn them that repeated failure of the child may lead to expulsion. The environment therefore is not conducive for education of children.

The chapter would emphasize mainly on inclusive education, which is a vital step towards inclusion. It would attempt to look at the philosophy, perspectives and initiatives for inclusive education in international and national context. There would also be an endeavour to elucidate the meaning and implication of inclusive education on all learners. The discussion would encompass some requisites in inclusive education that illustrate how to strengthen processes of inclusion in school settings.

The concept of inclusive education could only be operationalised once the philosophy behind it is understood. It is quite evident that an unbothered mainstream would not be able to guarantee equality of opportunities to all the learners. Inclusion requires a transformation of the ideology. Inclusive education is part of the strategic intervention. The aim of inclusive education is not only to cater to all learners but also to resist exclusionary pressures. Inclusion means much more than integration, it signifies that the disabled child is provided a similar environment and experiences as his/her typically developing peers. A better understanding of the inclusion philosophy would help us gain clarity on the subject matter and facilitate accreditation of the inclusion processes.

The Inclusion Philosophy

All individuals in their lives have sometime or the other felt excluded and neglected, in a way they all undergone the pain of being excluded from a group. The feeling of exclusion is difficult to put in words but it is not difficult to empathize with people who are victims of exclusion in all spheres of life.

When an individual finds that significant decisions affecting his/her life are taken out of his hands, the feeling of powerlessness that results may affect his sense of self worth and his ability to learn and achieve. When the child acquaints oneself with the fact that he/she may only be able to attend school with other disabled children, a feeling of inferiority develops in him/her. Others endow the status of being 'special' on the child. The word 'special' is no way special; it signifies that the child would be segregated from most other children throughout his/her life (Epstein, 1984). This segregation reinforces their belief that they need help for everything. They never get a chance to decide for themselves as others always force their decisions on them. The child loses his/her battle of autonomy even before starting it. Those who are not free to know, to learn and to interact with different kinds of people cannot achieve what Abraham Maslow called self actualization (1954). It is, therefore essential to enable the children with disabilities to live a normal life by granting and protecting their basic human rights. Inclusion ensures provision of equal opportunities to all learners irrespective of their abilities. It is a developmental approach, which disregards exclusion of any kind and indicative of a progressive society that cares for all its citizens.

Inclusion gears towards restructuring of the cultures, policies and practices in schools so that they respond to the diversity of students in their communities. Inclusion is concerned with the learning and participation of all students, not only those with impairments or those who are categorised as having 'special educational needs'. Inclusion within the educational system is a right for all learners and that neither parents nor professionals have the right to choose segregation for their children. Inclusion proponents argue that our schools must mirror this inclusive and diverse society (Gartner and Lipsky, 1987; Giangreco and Putnam, 1991).

The philosophy of inclusion rests on certain values. Firstly, there has to be no minimum criterion that a disabled child has to fulfil before the child could be accepted by the mainstream. The child does not have to constantly endeavour to reach the normal standards. An inclusive society adapts itself to meet the needs of all its citizens irrespective of their abilities. It gives to all its citizens a fulfilling experience, which would enable them to actualize their potential. It would mean a barrier free environment. Secondly, it also signifies accommodation of all people in a pluralistic society. The normal children have as much to learn from the disabled children as they have to learn from them. Thirdly, any programme or policies for the disabled children would require collaborative efforts from all participants. Also, inclusion means respecting each person's uniqueness and dignity. Inclusion places the burden of proof on the school to justify removal rather than on the child to justify why he or she should be allowed to return to regular education environments.

The inclusion philosophy has come about after several years of struggle and discrimination faced by the disabled people all over the world. Hence it would be significant to know how this perspective has evolved over time.

Changing Perspectives: Charity to Rights

In the past, children with disabilities were considered a social threat, which were believed to taint the otherwise pure human race. They were either exterminated or used as objects of entertainment by the community. Philanthropists concerned by their plight, advocated for their institutionalization. The disabled children were placed in asylums where their basic needs were taken care of by the staff. Asylums were not meant to be educational institutions (Bender, 1970). Special schools emerged in the 19th century, starting with those with sensory impairments. The special schools emphasized mainly on vocational skills. The curriculum followed in a special school varied considerably from the normal schools. This approach where the children with disabilities were viewed as victims of impairments and as the beneficiaries of charity, alms and services is referred to as the charitable approach to disability. Disabled children were viewed as tragic or suffering people to be pitied and cared for. Services are designed for them and delivered to them with the best of intentions, but with insufficient consultation. The special schools symbolize the existence of charitable and medical model of disability. The medical model tends to view disabled people first and foremost as having physical problems to be cured. The disabled person is relegated the passive role of patient, the medical personnel and care professionals making many decisions. It perceives disability as a problem located in the individual, and assumes that working on the individual can solve it. The disabled person becomes defined solely in terms of his/her diagnosis, and a patient with medical needs and not as a person with whole range of needs.

The cure to the problem of disability lies in the restructuring of society, unlike medically based 'cures', which focus on the individual and their impairment, this is an achievable goal and to the benefit of everyone. This approach is referred to as the 'social model' of disability. The social model of disability recognises that some people have impairments which affect how they function physically or mentally. But those people are disabled by the barriers that exist in a society that does not take account of their needs. These barriers may be in the physical, organisational or personal aspects of society - for instance, stairs without lifts, information not available in large print, or people's negative attitudes. The social model sees disabled people as having the same wants, needs and aspirations to non-disabled people. Disabled people should enjoy the same freedom and choices as those who are non-disabled and be allowed equal responsibility in determining their life choices.

This paradigm shift came with the concept of normalization, first developed in the Scandinavian countries particularly Denmark and Sweden in 1960s. Wolfensberger (1972) defined normalisation as, "Utilisation of means which are as culturally normative as possible, in order to establish and/or maintain personal behaviours and characteristics which are as culturally normative as possible". The scenario changed dramatically following the designation of 1981 as the International Year of Disabled Persons and when the United Nations General Assembly adopted the World Programme of Action Concerning Disabled Persons. It strongly encouraged the inclusive practices in education. In 1987, the Programme was reviewed, and human rights of persons with disabilities was recommended as a guiding philosophy for the World Programme. Another landmark in the education and care of the disabled children was the promulgation of the Convention on the Rights of the Child (CRC) in 1990, which recognized that a child with disability should enjoy a full and decent life, in conditions which ensure dignity, promote self-reliance and facilitate the child's active participation in the community. These and other international developments recognized and upheld the social model of disability which emerged out of the disability rights movement in Europe and in the United States of America in the 1970s and 1980s.

Since the 1980s, the disability rights perspective had become the dominant perspective adopted by leaders of the disability community and had been reflected in their approach to public policy. The rights-based approach to disability essentially means viewing persons with disabilities as subjects of law. Its final aim is to empower disabled persons, and to ensure their active participation in political, economic, social, and cultural life in a way that is respectful and accommodating of their difference. This approach is normatively based on international human rights standards and operationally directed to enhancing the promotion and protection of the human rights of persons with disabilities.

The right of every child to education is proclaimed in the Convention on the Rights of the Child (1989) and was cogently reaffirmed by the World Declaration on Education for All (1990). There is an emerging consensus that children with disabilities should be included in the educational arrangements made for the majority of children. This has led to the concept of the inclusive school. The challenge confronting the inclusive school is that of developing a child-centred pedagogy capable of successfully educating all children, including those who have serious disadvantages and disabilities. The merit of such schools is not only that they are capable of providing quality education to all children; their establishment is a crucial step in helping to change discriminatory attitudes, in creating welcoming communities and in developing an inclusive society (UNESCO, 1994). The proposed transformation of the educational system to accommodate all learners has generated a great debate between the advocates of existing special education system and proponents of inclusion. Thus, it is imperative to look at the viewpoints to develop a clearer understanding of the advantages and challenges of inclusive education.

The Debate: Inclusion *versus* Special Education

Inclusion is contentious proposal in education as it advocates for equality of all learners irrespective of their abilities. The movement towards inclusion has led to formation of two professional camps in the field of education of children with disabilities: one advocating for inclusion and the other supporters of special education. The advocates of the inclusion philosophy reject the supremacy of professionals as decision-makers and view disability as an interaction with the society and the environment rather than as a medical condition or physical or mental impairment. The latter believes that disabled children have certain special needs, which cannot be, met, in a regular classroom. The question here however is not taking a stand rather understanding that the two positions fall along a continuum. On one end are those advocating for "full inclusion" for every student and those who advocate for preservation of the current special education system on the other. Every other point along the continuum encourages various levels of inclusion while still maintaining some aspects of segregated programme.

Consequently, according to full inclusion advocates, it is very seldom, if ever, appropriate for a special education student to be outside the mainstream classroom setting. On the other hand, there are inclusion supporters who believe that numerous intervening variables make such an absolutist stand to be dangerous and irresponsible. According to them, the unique nature of individual disabilities, the school context, the capacity of teachers in terms of training and experience, and the availability of resources should all be taken into consideration before determining appropriate placement. However, they believe that all schools should be moving towards the greater inclusion of students with disabilities into mainstream classroom settings.

Those who prefer to maintain special education for students in resource rooms, special classrooms, or other, more restrictive settings believe that labelling students is not bad if the labels are accurate and lead to providing appropriate services. They believe that students with disabilities are distinctly different from their non-disabled peers and, therefore, need different, specialized services. They fear that the reason many are "pushing" inclusion is to save money (special education services are costly). Inclusion opponents believe that special education identification services are sophisticated and generally reliable. It is also believed that many or most students with disabilities are better served outside the mainstream classroom setting because:

- special education teachers have higher expectations for their students;
- special education curricula are appropriate for their intended students;
- individualization is more likely to occur in smaller classes with specialized teachers than in the regular classroom;
- regular teachers do not want special needs students in their classrooms; and
- students with disabilities have never been well-served in regular education, and there is nothing to indicate that teachers are any more able to deal with them now than they were previously. (Huebert,1994 as cited in Thompkins and Deloney, 1995).

In this regard, Hallahan and Kauffman (1994) conclude that no matter whose point of view prevails, it is fair to say that there will be dramatic changes over the next few years in how and especially where we educate students with disabilities. It may be useful to cite some researches conducted in the field of special and inclusive education which have clarified some important issues regarding efficacy and relevance.

There have been quite a few studies which have thrown light on the various aspects of special and inclusive education. What has been of much importance are the researches which have measured the efficacy of these systems on education of children with disabilities.

A study by Johnson (1962) revealed that children with special educational needs could not accomplish the objectives of education at the same rate and levels as similar students who had remained in general education classes. Another study conducted by Goldstein, Jordan and Moss (1965) where students were randomly assigned to special education or general education classes, showed no differences when their performance on academic achievement and tests of social knowledge were compared. Such studies offer an exceptional support to inclusive education.

In a qualitative study by Stainback and Stainback (1991) had reported the following in terms of resultant effect of inclusion in normal school.

- Change evokes fear among some classroom teachers and classmates, which generally subside with experience.
- Most difficulties are related to behaviour problems.
- Included students showed gains in learning.
- Included students had positive influences on their classmates.
- The mainstream curriculum requires adaptation.
- Collaboration and support are integral to inclusion.
- Social interactions varied among students, some positive and some negative.

In a study conducted by Cannon (1992) and colleagues it was determined that teachers in general and special education agreed on 82 per cent of essential teaching practices for effective instruction of children with disabilities. If what both special and general education teachers do for children with disabilities is essentially identical, many conclude that it is illogical to support segregated programming, especially if there are no significant differences in achievement.

If the results are closely examined there is an indication of positive influence of inclusion on both children with disabilities and their typically developing peers. In almost all the abovementioned researches, there are support evidences for inclusion. Benefits of inclusion for the general education student include: a curriculum that is more flexible and responsive to individualized needs, the presence of support services and technology, the collaboration of additional teaching experts in the classroom, and improved teacher training and teaching techniques. The research of Goodlad and Lovitt (1993) and Oakes and Lipton (1990) and others have clearly demonstrated that all students learn best when cooperative learning, problem solving, active participation of the students, and an accommodation of individual learning styles are utilized in the public schools. These teaching strategies are required in an inclusionary school because they encourage students to work hard and take risks. Students are more likely to take risks because inclusion fosters an environment that requires "a sense of community among faculty and students, a shared mission, and the ability to successfully collaborate with others" (Lyman, 1993).

In an inclusionary setting, students with special educational needs learn social skills and independence. In addition, the realization by the child with special educational needs that his schooling is not separate from siblings permits a more normal life for all family members and eventually more normalized functioning as an adult in the community. However, making the conventional schools inclusive is a daunting task and involves responses at all levels of the school functioning.

Making Conventional Schools Inclusive

Effective schooling systems are academically inclusive in nature. This shows, not only in their performance, but also in their ethos and their willingness to offer new opportunities to pupils who may have experienced previous difficulties. Hegarty (1993) spelled out requisite changes to be brought in regular schools in order to bring about inclusion :

- *Curriculum:* What is taught, with particular reference to establishing a balance between offerings a mainstream curriculum framework and taking account of individual needs.
- *Pedagogy:* How it is taught, again with reference to providing specialist support without isolating people from peers.
- *Academic organization:* How the school organizes itself to deliver curriculum effectively to the widest possible range of pupils by means of appropriate pupil grouping, arrangements for supplementary teaching and timetable construction.
- *Staffing:* Teachers, classroom assistants and support staff, all to be deployed flexibly, but with a shared dynamic focus on achieving 'school for all'.
- *Professional Development:* Essential underpinning of any school reform, to encompass attitude change, increased understanding and skill development.
- *Parental Involvement:* Collaboration to include sharing of information, involvement in curriculum delivery, parent support and liaison with professional agencies.

- *External Support:* Special schools and support agencies to provide essential input - training, assessment, curriculum planning, therapy - but without usurping the school's principal responsibility.

As has been stated earlier, the most fundamental prerequisite for inclusion in reform and restructuring of ordinary schools. An index of inclusion had been devised by Booth and Ainscow (2000) in order to enable the schools to carry out a self-evaluation of problems in developing inclusive practice. The Index for Inclusion is a set of materials to guide schools through a process of inclusive school development. It is about building supportive communities and fostering high achievement for all staff and students.

The school could use the Index to:

- adopt a self-review approach to analyse their cultures, policies and practices and to identify the barriers to learning and participation that may occur within each of these areas.
- decide their own priorities for change and to evaluate their progress.
- use it as an integral part of existing development policies, encouraging a wide and deep scrutiny of everything that makes up a school's activities.

The Index takes the social model of disability as its starting point, builds on good practice, and then organises the Index work around a cycle of activities which guide schools through the stages of preparation, investigation, development and review.

Another significant aspect of inclusive education is effective cross disciplinary collaboration. Collaboration is an ongoing style of interaction in which people voluntary engage in shared programme planning, implementation, evaluation and overall programme accountability (Bauwens and Hourcade, 1995 as cited in Alper *et al.*, 1995). In order to successfully implement collaborative programmes, the customary roles and responsibilities need to be transformed. There needs to be a modification of the teaching techniques, course content, evaluation and grading procedures to accommodate all students with diverse needs. It is important for the collaborative team to know about the functional information about the child and his/her skills and effect of instruction of those skills. The best way to get this information is through use of curriculum based measures (Shinn and Hubbard, 1992). Curriculum-based Measurement (CBM), as developed by Deno (1985) and colleagues used repeated measures from the student's curriculum to evaluate the effectiveness of instruction and instructional changes to lead to more effective teaching methods and improved student achievement.

Some of mentioned structural, administrative and attitudinal transformations and efforts by the collaborative teams could lead to successful inclusionary practices. The society has come a long way from extermination of the disabled children in the primitive era to their inclusion in the society. The chapter would now examine some important international developments that have led to this progressive change.

Inclusive Education: International Developments

A glance at some significant developments in the developed nations particularly in UK and US which have influenced the international initiatives and developments in the field of Inclusive Education is essential at this juncture. The chapter thus attempts to construct a sequential overview of inclusionary practices in the West.

The idea of 'normalization' was developed in Scandinavia in the 1960s. It aimed towards providing a pattern of life as normal as possible. Normalization implied that almost all disabled people would live in the community, participate in the normal activities and relationships, experiencing choices, and having full access to social and educational opportunities. This may be regarded as an initial step towards inclusion of people with special needs in the society.

The Warnock Committee Report, UK, 1978 highlighted the importance of educating children in their crucial years and placed education of disabled children amongst its top priorities. It is well established that for all children the early (0-5 years) are crucial for an all-round development. When we say "all" we mean disabled children as well. In fact inadequate stimulation at the crucial age may prove more disastrous for disabled children than normal children. At this age, the disabled children stand a better chance to improve abilities. It is therefore suggested that this period could be utilized optimally by parents and teachers to prevent permanent retardation or secondary disabilities. The Education Act of 1981 in UK also emphasized the importance of integrated education for disabled children. It reiterated that no disabled child should be sent to a special school who can satisfactorily be educated in an ordinary school.

In USA, the difference to the education of the disabled was made by launching of "Head Start", an education programme by President Lyndon Johnson in 1964. The most unique characteristic of the programme was that it admitted disabled children as well. The programme aimed at holistic development of children and was regarded as one of the largest preschool programmes across the globe. In 1975, the Education for All Disabled Children was enacted which mandated free, equal and appropriate public education to all children and young people with special needs in the age group of 3 and 21. There are three federal laws that protect individuals with disabilities and ensure their rights to educational opportunities with non-disabled peers (Inos and Quigley, 1995). The first one is Section 504 of the Rehabilitation Act of 1973. The law required that each school educate the disabled students in their jurisdiction unless the school can prove that the child's needs cannot be met in the general classroom. The second federal law is the Individuals with Disabilities Education Act, (IDEA). In 1975, IDEA introduced the legal concepts of the "Individualized Education Plan" (IEP) and least restrictive environment. This law guaranteed that disabled students needs will be identified and met in the classroom, or if this is not possible, provided as near to the student's home and in the least restrictive environment possible. The third federal law, the Americans with Disabilities Act of 1990 (ADA), provides a clear and comprehensive national mandate for the elimination of discrimination against individuals with disabilities. It guarantees equal opportunity for individuals with disabilities in employment, public accommodations (including most private schools, child care centres, etc.), transportation, State and local government services (including public schools), and telecommunications.

Internationally, the drive towards inclusion was fuelled by a number of initiatives and treaties, including the UN Convention on the Rights of the Child (1989), the UN Standard Rules on the Equalisation of Opportunities for Persons with Disabilities (1993) and the UNESCO Salamanca Statement (1994). All of these documents recognise the human right perspective and promote equal opportunity for education to all children.

The rights of children with disabilities to be educated in the mainstream were spelled out for the first time in United Nations Convention on the Rights of the Child. Article 23 of the Convention calls for a child to be educated in a way that will allow him or her to achieve the 'fullest possible social integration and individual development'. The UN Committee on the Rights of the Child has since interpreted this as a goal for inclusion for all children. Article 2 says that all rights in the Convention shall apply to all children without discrimination - and it specifically mentions disability. Articles 3, 6, 12, 28 and 29 in the Convention give further support to inclusive education for all disabled children.

Among the major outcomes of the Decade of Disabled Persons was the adoption, by the General Assembly, of the Standard Rules on the Equalization of Opportunities for Persons with Disabilities in 1993. Although not a legally binding instrument, the Standard Rules represent a strong moral and political commitment of Governments to take action to attain equalization of opportunities for persons with disabilities. The rules serve as an instrument for policy-making and as a basis for technical and economic cooperation. Rule 6 of the Rules pertains to Education. It asserts that States should recognize the principle of equal primary, secondary and tertiary educational opportunities for children, youth and adults with disabilities, in integrated settings. They should ensure that the education of persons with disabilities is an integral part of the educational system.

Another major landmark in the field of inclusive education was adoption of the SALAMANCA STATEMENT by the World Conference on Special Needs Education in June 1994. The idea was to uphold the aim of 'Education for All' by suggesting some basic changes in programmes and policies. In order to serve all children it advocated for inclusive education and laid the responsibility of education the children with disabilities with the nation's government. The Conference organized by the Government of Spain and UNESCO, adopted the Salamanca Statement on Principles, Policy and Practice in Special Needs Education and a Framework for Action.

The outstanding features of the Salamanca Statement are that it honours the differences in abilities of learners and supports inclusive education. It emphasizes that every child has a basic right to education and every child has unique characteristics, interests, abilities and learning needs. It is, therefore, the duty of the educational service provider to cater to these diverse characteristics and needs. There needs to be a greater accessibility of regular schools to children with special educational needs. It believes that regular schools with an inclusive ethos are the most effective way to combat discriminatory attitudes, create welcoming and inclusive communities and achieve education for all. Such inclusive schools provide effective education to the majority of children; improve efficiency and cost-effectiveness.

The responsibility of realizing the goal of achieving "Education for All" lies with the governments of nations. The Salamanca Statement solicits governments to give the highest priority to making education systems inclusive and adopt the principle of inclusive education as a matter of law or policy. It further recommends that the government must take the lead and develop demonstration projects. The exchange programmes with countries having successful experience of inclusion must be encouraged. It must set up ways to plan, monitor and evaluate educational provision for children and adults. The participation of parents and organizations of disabled people must be encouraged and made easy. There have to investments in early identification and intervention strategies and vocational aspects of inclusive education. Another area to be developed and strengthened is the teacher training programmes.

The document on Framework for Action outlined new thinking on special needs education and guidelines for action at national, regional and international levels. The nation's course of action would be to restructure policy and organization, adequate equipment of the school in terms of infrastructure and staff, recruitment and training of the educational personnel, defining priority areas and building community perspectives.

These global initiatives have caused the member nations to promulgate policies and programmes for children with disabilities in their countries. This places an obligation on the member nations to comply with the international ideology and standards for safeguarding the rights of the disabled populace of the world. The chapter would now examine some major developments towards inclusive education in India.

National Initiatives for Inclusive Education

Due to insufficient documentation the researchers are poorly informed about India's special educational needs and disability issues in the nineteenth century (Alur, 2002). Integrated education was conceptualized by the Royal Commonwealth Society for the Blind and the Christopher Blind Mission during the nineteenth century, though the efforts were not full hearted. The visually impaired children were integrated in regular classrooms where they were expected to pick up whatever they could during the classroom sessions where oral repetition was the dominant pedagogy (Chaddha, 2003). Until about 1947, the provincial governments had taken sporadic interest in education and training of the disabled by giving *ad hoc* grants to the schools and institutions run by the voluntary sector (Gupta, 1984 as cited in Alur, 2002).

During the post-independence period the Ministry of Education launched a comprehensive scholarship scheme in 1952; a rudimentary beginning of the integrated education initiative by the Government. The first time the issue of education of children with disabilities was raised by the Kothari Commission, 1964. The report categorically mentioned that the Constitutional directive on compulsory education includes children with disabilities. It clearly stated that the education of children with disabilities should not be undertaken as a welfare activity, instead of promoting social justice. This aspect of the report though was unrecognized during implementation through policies and programmes.

Learning from the international developments in the field of inclusive education, India launched its scheme of Integrated Education for Disabled Children, popularly known as the IEDC in 1974. The aim of the scheme was to provide children with special needs opportunities for education in regular schools and to facilitate their retention in the schools. The scope of the scheme included pre-school training, counselling for the parents, and special training in skills for all kinds of disabilities. The scheme provided facilities in the form of books, stationery, uniforms, and allowances for transport, reader, escort etc. The responsibility of educating children with special needs (CWSN) rested only with the Central Government. No sooner did the Central Government convert the scheme to dual sharing between the centre and the states in 1979 than the states discontinued the scheme (Jangira, 2002). Hence, the scheme met only with limited success. Due to the inability of the government to cater to the diverse learning needs of the CWSN, the task of educating the children with special needs was entrusted to the non-governmental organization in most states. This resulted in localized action and limited coverage of the children with disabilities.

To strengthen the implementation of the IEDC scheme the Project on Integrated Education for the Disabled (PIED), with UNICEF assistance was introduced in 1987. The project was undertaken in selected blocks of ten states. The National Council of Education Research and Training (NCERT) provided the teachers with special training to manage children with special needs in the regular classrooms. An external evaluation illustrated that not only did the enrolment of disabled children increased considerably, their dropout rates decreased to a great extent.

(Dasgupta, 2002). It had a positive impact on learning of children with special needs, created awareness about integration of CWSN in regular classrooms and gave an opportunity to the regular teachers to handle diversity in their classrooms. The project fostered integration and resulted in high enrolment of children with special needs in the regular classroom.

Taking positive cues from the shifting ideology of Integration to Inclusion in the international scenario, India launched the District Primary Education Programme (DPEP) in 1994. It was in pursuance of the 'Education for All' philosophy propagated at the Salamanca Conference, to which India was a signatory. The Ministry of Social Justice and Empowerment, in the Eighth Five Year Plan, 1991-1996, increased the budget for children with impairments by more than five times (DPEP, 1993).

Another constructive step by our country towards inclusion of disabled people in the communites was promulgation of the Persons with Disabilities (Equal Opportunities, Protection of Rights and Full Participation) Act, 1995 to give effect to the Proclamation on the Full Participation and Equality of the People with Disabilities in the Asian and Pacific Region adopted by the Economic and Social Commission for Asia and Pacific held at Beijing on 1st to 5th December, 1992. Even though the new legislation (The Person with Disability Act, 1995) made access to regular schools easier, it is still not guaranteed as an equal right for all students. Segregation into separate special schools breaches the underlying principles of the United Nations Convention on the Rights of the Child (1989) yet the Government still sanctions the exclusion of significant numbers of children. This contradictory situation is a barrier to the assumption by regular schools of full responsibility for all students in their areas.

Most recent advancement is the promulgation of the National Policy for Persons with Disability, 2006, which attempts to clarify the framework under which the state, civil society and private sector must operate in order to ensure a dignified life for persons with disability and support for their caregivers. It includes : extending rehabilitation services to rural areas, increasing trained personnel to meet needs, emphasising education and training, increasing employment opportunities, focusing on gender equality, improving access to public services, encouraging state governments to develop a comprehensive social security policy, ensuring equal opportunities in sports, recreation and cultural activities, increasing the role of civil society organisations as service-providers to persons with disability and their families.

The Figure 4.1 attempts a comparison between the doctrines of the international statutes and its compliance by our country government. India being a signatory to a number of international treaties and conventions which uphold the equal status of the disabled and places responsibility on the member nations to ensure that their social, economic, cultural and political rights are protected. The legislation, The Person with Disability Act, 1995 and the National Policy for Persons with Disability, 2006 are reflections of the international commitment towards equal opportunities for the persons with disabilities in India, though the implementation of these policies and legislations is questionable. These rules clearly spell out the promotion of inclusive education practice which by far is a neglected area. The response to the educational needs of children with disabilities has been extended to various categories rather than providing for the diversity that exists. The national institutes as well as the special schools are meant for specific categories of the disabled children. It defies the basic spirit of inclusive education which aims to cater to the diverse needs of learners under one roof.

Ratification of international covenants call for commitment and action at three levels: legislative, financial and ideological. Whenever an act or policy is enacted following ratification of a convention, its implementation depends on the financial and ideological commitment the nation's government shows towards change. The Indian government has developed four national level institutes. However, the prime objective of these institutes is rehabilitation. They are not involved with education and delivery of services. Though the government relies heavily on the voluntary sector for provision of basic facilities for education, it has allocated only 30 per cent of the planned expenditure on the voluntary sector and the rest is reserved for the national institutes and factories it has set for aids and appliances (Alur, 2002). This indicates that the priorities of our government are different to those upheld by the international covenants. The issues and practice of inclusive education take a back seat and what continues is the prevalence of segregated educational environment.

The international statutes uphold the social model of disability and reject the charitable model or construction of disability as a problem located in the disabled individual who possesses medical needs. A high proportion of social welfare policies and traditional charities subscribe to the medical point of view, in which disabled people are rendered dependent passive recipients of charity (Chib, 2002). Though in legislations, there is a mention of inclusive practices and ensuring rights and independence to the children with disabilities, the practice shows coexistence of these social, medical and charitable perspectives. The international policies aim towards equity and equal opportunities of disabled people in all spheres, their translation at national level has been reduced to integration of those disabled children who are educable, as assessed by the team of professionals.

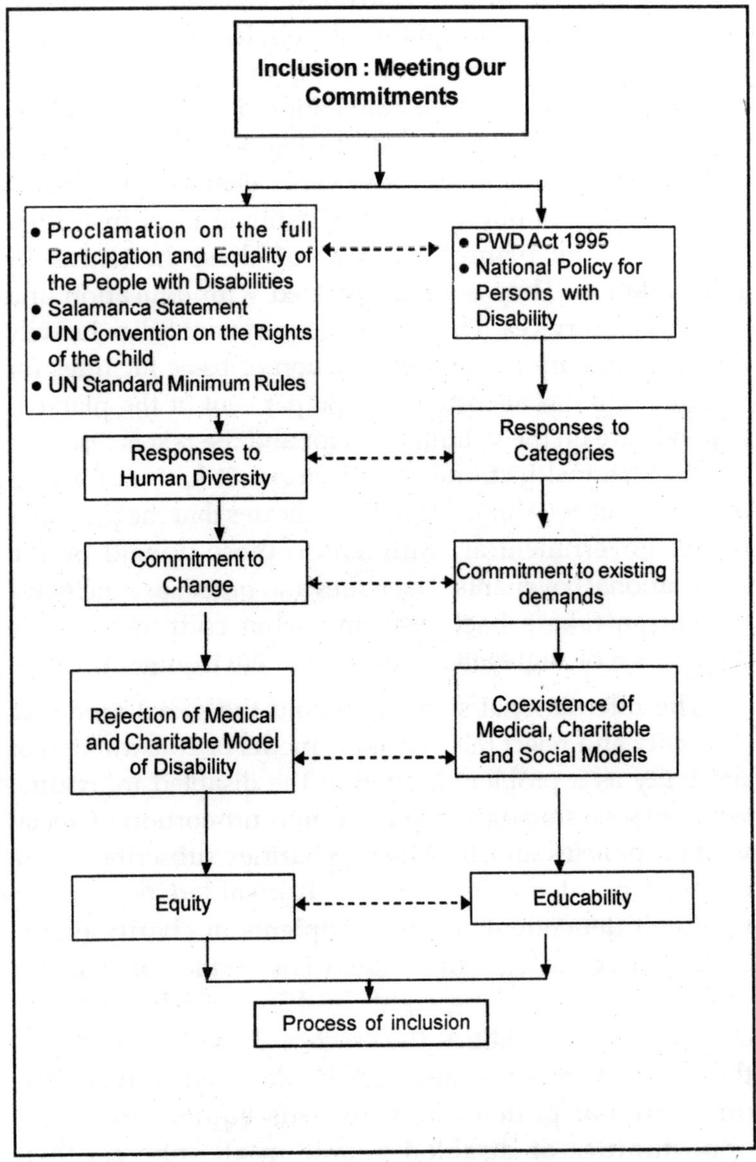

Figure 4.1: Inclusion: Its translation in the Indian Context

Source : Adapted and modified from: Jelas, Z.M. (2000).

So far the chapter has dealt with the philosophy and initiatives in the field of inclusive education, it would now highlight some effective practices either suggested or working in inclusive educational settings.

Towards Effective Inclusion

The existing system of segregated education of disabled children has augmented the gap between regular and special schools. Research supports the fact that educating disabled children in pull-out programmes is not a viable approach to education. There is also enough research evidence to prove that the children with disabilities could be educated effectively in regular schools if appropriate practices and methods are used (Banerjee and Daily, 1995; Bishop, 1995).

This chapter would highlight some effective practices in inclusionary settings particularly, classroom management and school reform. Education system is strictly examination oriented, high pressured and fiercely competitive. The proposal of educating non-disabled and children with special needs in one classroom is often considered impossible under such circumstances. The regular teachers are trained in a way that they remain indifferent to the needs of special children in class.

Pre-service preparation of the teachers is of paramount importance in inclusive education. The model suggested by Whitworth (1999) for inclusive teacher training takes into account the differences in abilities of learners in the classroom. In order to address this diversity within the classrooms the Whitworth's model focuses on two dimensions; outcomes of the model and specific programme components.

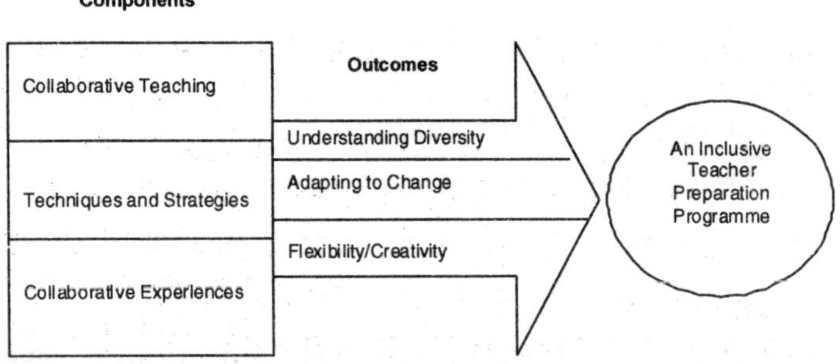

Figure 4.2: An Inclusive Teacher Preparation Model

Source: Whitworth, 1999.

The specifics of the teacher training programme components have been illustrated in Figure 4.2. A very essential part is the Collaborative Teaching Component. The educators collaborate for teaching, planning and evaluation. The approaches as collaborative learning arrangements and activities requiring students to develop and practice group process skills could prove beneficial for the classroom. Another component is the instructional techniques and strategies that the teachers must possess for teaching in diverse settings. Pre-service preparation must address appropriate accommodations in curriculum, instructional activities and evaluation procedures, effective identification, development and utilization of resources and various instructional arrangements such as multi-level teaching, cooperative learning and peer tutoring. The last component is related to the field based experiences of the prospective teacher. The teachers must get the opportunity to work in collaborative inclusive settings.

The next segment of the model deals with the possible outcomes of the teacher's training. Reportedly, there is a narrow range of diversity with which the teacher is comfortable. It, therefore, makes it difficult to address the diverse needs within the inclusive classroom. It is important that the teachers are aware and trained to handle diversity in the classroom. Adaptability to change is another vital consequence of the programme. There is little doubt that the classrooms of the future would be governed by inclusivity rather than exclusivity. This positive change also demands flexibility and creativity on part of the teachers which could be enhanced/developed by providing experiential pre-service training to the teachers.

Trained teachers could without doubt make a difference in the inclusive classrooms. Other ways for bringing about effective inclusion in the classrooms is implementing some pre-designed models. Many models have been suggested and practiced for achieving the goal of inclusive education in the classroom. Gartner and Lipsky (1997) had reported three working models for effective inclusion. Where the number of children with special needs is less in a regular classroom, the Consultant Model could be opted. The consultant model requires the help of the special teacher to teach difficult skills to the children with special needs. The other model is named the Teaming Model that requires the special and regular teachers to function as a team. The special educator provides student information, possible instructional strategies, modification ideas for assignments/ tests, and behaviour strategies. The team meets on a regular basis, establishing consistent communication among the team members. Another model is called Collaborative or Co-teaching Model which entails perfect synchronization between special and regular educators as they are co-teachers. Both are responsible for instruction planning and delivery, student achievement, assessment, and discipline. Co-teaching is defined as two or more professionals delivering substantive instruction to a group of students with diverse learning needs. This approach increases instructional options, improves educational programmes, reduces stigmatization for students, and provides support to the professionals involved. Co-teaching is an appropriate service delivery approach for students with disabilities who can benefit from general education curriculum if given appropriate supports. Teachers and related service professionals who are flexible and have good judgement are likely to be successful in this role. Co-teachers need preparation, administrative support, and opportunities to nurture their collaborative relationships. Co-teaching programmes should be planned and implemented systematically. Deliberate and ongoing communication among everyone involved is essential (Cook & Friend, 1995). Though the implementation of models could prove beneficial for inclusive classrooms, the educators must remember that the effectiveness of the model lies in its translation in classroom contexts.

Inclusion is practically not so simple. The chapter has shown how every aspect of the inclusive education has to be looked into for effective inclusion. Be it the pre-service preparation or the implementation of the models within the classroom, all requires sustained efforts of the educators. Though educating the pupil is largely a responsibility of the educator, one cannot undermine the importance of the family in the educational process. Thus, Transdisciplinary teams assume great importance in inclusive settings.

Transdisciplinary functioning means professionals from different streams work together alongside the family members of the child. The transdisciplinary approach is recommended because it: (1) prevents the fragmentation of services along disciplinary lines, (2) avoids duplication of services, (3) views the whole child's development as integrated, and (4) emphasizes the importance of the family as equal, contributing members of the team (Losardo & Notari-Sylverson, 2001; McWilliam, 2000). The focus of the team is integrated development of the child and hence effective communication between team members becomes an indispensable component. The assessment, planning, intervention and monitoring require the team members to come together. This certainly means that team members must be willing to share their knowledge with each other and be open to acquiring new skills (McWilliam, 2000).

The main thrust of preparation for inclusion has been to prepare the general education teacher as well as the student with exceptionalities for this educational initiative. Students without disabilities are often not the prevailing focus in these efforts. The typically developing peers have a great role to play in inclusion. They must be aware and prepared for this prospect. As far as possible they must be involved in the classroom processes.

There is no perfect recipe for inclusion. There are however some requisites for inclusion. Each classroom has to be a community, which satisfies every child's need to belong. The child needs a response as an individual from the educators and his/her peers. The educator must focus on child's strengths. Co-operative learning should be a goal for all; there must be sincere attempts in classrooms, families and society to minimize competition and promote co-operation.

Conclusion

The international conventions on equalization of opportunity for the disabled, human rights for all and inclusive educations have set the ground for action by the ratifying countries. These conventions however have no legal binding on the countries. These international documents call for collective action in terms of translation of the vision into national policy. The developed nations apart from the ideological commitment have allocated sufficient funds towards meeting this directive of equal opportunity. In our country the Government has not translated the philosophy into action due to lack of commitment in ideological and financial terms.

There is no doubt that our country has witnessed a phenomenal expansion in the field of education but the children with disabilities have not profited much from the growth in educational sector. The education of the disabled children in India is more than a century old, but the services are far from adequate. Though the past two decades have seen an increase in the integrated education programmes, their numbers are dissatisfactory. It has been observed that educational institutions have not been able to even admit ten per cent of the educable children in the regular schools.

In our country programmes like poverty alleviation, caste and gender issues and rural upliftment take a higher priority. The disabled suffer to the maximum extent of marginalization. Inclusion of children with disabilities is achievable and it should be an ultimate priority. The inclusion concept acknowledges the diversity present among the children in the general classrooms and addresses the fact that every child is a special child. In addressing the challenges of educating these children, the schools become effective schools and the teachers become effective teachers. The inclusion philosophy guarantees equal rights to all children with special.

Central tasks for us, therefore, are to foster critical awareness of how, despite the rhetoric of inclusion, present legislative frameworks promote exclusive above inclusive values and to combat institutionalized discrimination through legislative reform. Other important areas of work include making links between the wide range of barriers faced by learners, teachers and others in schools, who may be excluded as a result of poverty, cultural background or gender, as well as by the competitive and selective procedures that increasingly characterise education in this country.

Inclusion is not simply placing children with disabilities in an ordinary school where minor changes have been made and hoping that everything will work out. The special schools exist because the ordinary schools have not been able to cater to the diverse learning needs of pupils. The task therefore is to bring about school reforms, which require a transformation at the system level in terms of changes in the admission criteria, staffing, curriculum and assessment, physical environment, financing, involvement of parents and external support.

There is an imperative need for our country to concurrently focus on the enrollment of children with disabilities and creating an enabling educational environment to support the inclusion process through review and adaptations in curricula, capacity building among various groups ranging from policy makers to education administrators, teachers and parents groups. Pre-service and in-service training of mainstream school teachers should be a prime focus with the disability component included in all teachers training programme. Policy reforms need greater clarity of the concept. Organisational and professional development issues must be acknowledged prior to inclusion. A holistic approach in school and commitment to policy initiatives are crucial to create an environment that promotes inclusion.

References

Alper S., Schloss, P.J., Etscheidt and Macfarlane, C.A. (1995). *Inclusion: Are We Abandoning or Helping Children?* California: Corwin Press Inc.

Alur, M. (2002). Special Needs Policy in India, in Seamus Hegarty and Mithu Alur (Eds.) *Education and Children with Special Needs - From Segregation to Inclusion*. New Delhi: Sage Publications Inc.

Banerji, M. and Daily, R.A. (1995). 'A Study of the Effects of an Inclusion Model on Students with Specific Learning Disabilities', *Journal of Learning Disabilities*, 28 (8), 511.

Bender, R. (1970). *The Conquest of Deafness*. Cleveland: Western Reserve University.

Bishop, M. (1995). Inclusion: Balancing the Ups and Downs, *Momentum*, 26 (3), 28-30.

Booth, T. and Ainscow, M. (2000). *Index for Inclusion: Developing Learning and Participation in Schools*. Bristol: Centre for Studies in Inclusive Education. http://www.inclusion.uwe.ac.uk

Cannon, G. (1992) Educating students with mild handicaps in general classrooms: Essential teaching practices for general and special educators. *Journal of Learning Disabilities*, 25(5) 300-317.

Chadha, A. (2003). Perspectives in Special Needs Education in India: A Journey from Isolation to Inclusion, *Janshala,* Volume VI, Issue 1 January-March 2003, Joint GOI-UN System Education Programme.

Cook, L., & Friend, M. (1995). Co-teaching: Guidelines for creating effective practices. *Focus on Exceptional Children.* Vol. 28 (3), Love Publishing Co

Dasgupta P.R. (2002). 'Education for the Disabled', in Seamus Hegarty and Mithu Alur (Eds.) *Education and Children with Special Needs - From Segregation to Inclusion.* New Delhi: Sage Publications Inc.

Deno, S. L. (1985). Curriculum-based measurement: The emerging alternative. *Exceptional Children,* 52, 219-232.

District Primary Education Programme (DPEP) (1993). *DPEP Guidelines. New Delhi: Ministry of Human Resource Development,* Government of India.

Epstein, C. (1984). *Special Children in Regular Classrooms: Mainstreaming Skills for Teachers.* USA: Reston Publishing Company, Inc., a Prentice Hall Company.

Gartner, A., & Lipsky, D.D. (1987). Beyond Special Education: Toward a quality System for all students, *Harvard Educational Review,* 57, 367-385.

Gartner, A., & Lipsky, D.D. (1997). *Inclusion and school reform: Transferring America's Classrooms.* Baltimore: P.H. Brookes Publishing.

Giangreco, M. and Putnam, J. (1991). Supporting the Education of Students with Severe Disabilities in Regular Education Environments, in L.H. Mayer, C. Peck, and L. Brown (Eds.) *Critical Issues in the Lives of the People with Severe Disabilities* (pp. 245-270). Baltimore: Paul H. Brookes.

Goldstein, H., Moss, J. and Jordon, L. (1965). *The efficacy of special class training on the development of mentally retarded children.* Urbana, Ill.:University of Illinois

Goodlad, J. I., & Lovitt, T. C. (Eds.). (1993). *Integrating general and special education.* New York: Merrill.

Hallahan, D.P. and Kauffman, J.M. (1994). *Exceptional Children: Introduction to Special Education.* Boston: Allyn and Bacon.

Hegarty, S. (1993). *Meeting Special Needs in Ordinary Schools: An Overview.* London: Cassell.

Inos, R.H., and Quigley, M.A. (1995). *Research Review for Inclusive Practice.* Honolulu, HI: Pacific Region Educational Lab.

Jangira, N.K. (2002). Special Educational Needs of Children and Young Adults: An Unfinished Agenda, in Seamus Hegarty and Mithu Alur (Eds.) *Education and Children with Special Needs - From Segregation to Inclusion.* New Delhi: Sage Publications Inc.

Johnson, G.O. (1962). Special educator for the mentally handicapped - A paradox. *Exceptional Children,* 29(2), 62- 69.

Losardo, A., & Notari-Sylverson, A. (2001). *Alternative Approaches to Assessing Young Children.* Baltimore: Brookes.

Lyman, L. (1993). *Group Building for Successful Inclusion Programmes.* Washington, DC: Flint Hills Educational Research Development Association Special Education Inclusion Conference.

Maslow, A. (1954). *Motivation and Personality.* NY: Harper.

McWilliam, R.A. (2000). Recommended practices in interdisciplinary models, in S. Sandall, M. McLean, & B. Smith (Eds.), *DEC recommended practices for early intervention/early childhood special education* (pp. 47-54). Longmont, CO: Sopris West.

Oakes, J. and Lipton, M. (1990). *Making the best of schools: A handbook for parents, teachers, and policymakers.* New Haven: Yale University Press

Price, B.J., Mayfield, P.K., McFadden, A.C., and Marsh, J.E. (2001) *Collaborative Teaching: Special Education for Inclusive Classrooms,* Parrot Publishing, L.L.C.

Shinn, M.R. and Hubbard, D.D. (1992). Curriculum-based-measurement and Problem-solving Assessment: Basic Procedures and Outcomes. Focus on Exceptional Children, 24, 1-20.

Stainback, S. & Stainback, W. (1991). Promoting inclusive education: What happened in one school. Quality Outcomes - Driven Education, December, 15-25.

Thompkins, R. and Deloney, (1995). *Inclusion: The Pros & Cons, Issues About Change.* Volume 4, Number 3. Southwest Educational Development Library.

UNESCO (1997) - at the UN-Committee on Rights of the Child, October 6, 1997 - Centre for Human Rights, Geneva.

UNESCO (1994). *The Salamanca Statement and Framework for Action on Special Needs Education.*

UNICEF (1989). *U.N. Convention on the Rights of the Child,* New York: UNICEF.

United Nations (1993). *The Standard Rules on the Equalization of Opportunities for Persons with Disabilities*. New York: United Nations.

Whitworth, J.W. (1999). 'A Model for Inclusive Teacher Preparation', *Electronic Journal of Inclusive Education Fall*, Vol. 1, Edn. 2, 1999 Ohio: Wright State University.

Wolfensberger, W. (1972). *Normalization: The Principle of Normalization in Human Services*. Toronto: National Institute on Mental Retardation.

Jelas, Zalizan M. (2000). *Inclusion: Equity or Educability?* Paper Presented at International Special Education Congress 2000, University of Manchester, 24th-28th July 2000.

5

INCLUSIVE EDUCATION
Lessons from High Income Nations

Introduction

The ideological basis for providing equal opportunities in education to all learners is the need to respond to a diversity of students in the light of social justice, equity and democratic participation (Clark et al., 1999). Indeed, the 'equal opportunity' approach is an international movement that advocates educating all students in regular classroom settings to the maximum extent possible irrespective of their differences in intellectual, physical, sensory or other characteristics. The international pronouncements in the recent years regarding the education of children with disabilities have been very encouraging. Amongst the covenants, the Convention on the Rights of the Child (1989), UN Standard Rules (1993), the UNESCO Salamanca Statement (1994), UN Convention on Rights of the Persons with Disabilities (2006) have been the major positive influences on the legislations concerning education of children with disabilities of the ratifying high income nations. All the covenants have stipulations supporting inclusive education, which provides equal opportunities to all students.

The other reasons which have considerably affected the education of children with disabilities in the high income countries is the need to promote economic growth, create employment opportunities, foster civic participation, greater tolerance, and peace and intercultural dialogue. The impact of keeping children with disabilities at home denying them education and rendering them economically inactive later, as well as family members who are unable to work due to caring responsibilities, all contribute significantly to the impoverishment of disabled people and their families.

All over the world, the trend is towards the development of free market economies and globalization; this is accompanied by an awareness of the importance of education and training. The enhanced focus on "education for all" (Dakar Framework for Action, 2000) for the cause of development has led to an understanding of the educational needs of the vulnerable sections of the society like children with disabilities as well. It is important to acknowledge that education for disabled children is not only a fundamental human right but is also essential for the alleviation of poverty and sustainable development. According to Metts (2000), the estimated annual value of Gross Domestic Product (GDP) lost as a result of disability globally is 1936 billion US Dollars (Table 5.1). The study was conducted in 207 countries by extrapolating the results of research which estimated the GDP lost due to disability in Canada (the Canadian Study) to the rest of the world using UNDP's unemployment rate estimates and GDP estimates for the other 206 nations. This is indicative of the high population of the people with disabilities and their inability to contribute to the country's economy due to lack of educational and employment resources for them.

Table 5.1 :Total Annual Value of GDP Lost Due to Disability (in US Dollars)

Value of GDP Lost	High Estimate	Low Estimate
High Income Countries	1,264,232,430,105	891,283,863,224
Medium Income Countries	480,206,038,845	338,545,257,386
Low Income Countries	192,002,986,035	135,362,105,155
Total	$1,936,441,454,95	$1,65,191,225,765

Source : R.L. Metts (2000 : 8)

Children with disabilities have long suffered educational discrimination and segregation all over the world. They have progressed from neglect, to institutions, to residential schooling and other isolated schools and classes, to pull-out programmes and mainstreaming and are continuing in the direction of full inclusion. The past two decades have seen tremendous changes in the way the educational programmes are conceptualized for them all over the world. In order to ensure the right of children with disabilities to an inclusive education and mitigate the sustained poverty resulting from their exclusion, it is vital to recognize that all children can learn, transform the existing education systems, promote inclusive environments, prioritise teacher training and ensure that funding promotes education for disabled children.

The educational system for children with disabilities that exists today has been influenced by myriad factors. As education has evolved it has been shaped by the legislations, the civil rights movement and changing social and political beliefs. The review of literature, current statistics and international policy statements underscore the urgency of raising the inclusion of children with disabilities to a high priority in all proposed actions and programmes in order to attain the highest equitable educational standards. This has been reflected well in the policies and programmes on education for the children with disabilities in the high income countries where the policies have got adequate financial support resulting in superior action and implementation. Even mere glimpses of the historical developments in education for children with disabilities indicate a proactive influence of the western countries.

Some of the philosophies and perspectives which have tremendously affected the educational system had originated and nurtured in the West. The idea of 'normalization' was developed in Scandinavia in the 1960s. It aimed towards providing a pattern of life as normal as possible. Normalization implied that almost all disabled people would live in the community, participate in the normal activities and relationships, experiencing choices, and having full access to social and educational opportunities. Amongst other landmark developments in the field of education of children with special needs is the Warnock Committee Report, UK, 1978 which highlighted the importance of educating children in their crucial years and placed education of disabled children amongst its top priorities. An initiative in a similar direction in USA was made by launching of "Head Start", an education programme by President Lyndon Johnson in 1964. The most unique characteristic of the programme was that it admitted disabled children as well.

The high income nations have lead the battle against the discrimination of disabled children and contributed a great deal in development of the global statutes. The international drive towards recognizing and safeguarding the rights of the children with disabilities brought about a sea change in the policies and action initiatives for them in various countries. For instance, there has been a strong movement in the last 20 years in Australia towards educating students with disabilities in mainstream schools and in mainstream classes. In 2002, the majority of children with disabilities attended mainstream rather than special schools; 81 per cent of children with disabilities attending government schools and 91 per cent of children with disabilities attending non-government schools were in mainstream settings (AIHW, 2004).

It was therefore essential to develop a comprehensive knowledge base of the current developments in the high-income nations on education of children with special needs so as to help in construction of a contextual model for our country. Out of the 56 high income nations, the chapter would look at policies and programmes for education of the children with disabilities in two countries; United Kingdom and United States of America. These countries have been selected because of couple of reasons; the 'disability rights movement' was initiated in these two countries and that they are known to have a relatively older history of special education than other countries. The chapter would examine the policy provisions and action initiatives in the field of education of children with special needs in the two countries. There would be an endeavour to present a comparative analysis of the two countries thus bringing out issues related to success or failure of the special/inclusive education services for the children with disabilities.

Education of Children with Disabilities in America

The development of special education in the United States during the 1960s owes its credit to the involvement of the federal government under the active leadership of President Kennedy. He was the main force behind the generating public awareness about disability and giving it a policy form (Osgood, 2005). According to the Report published by American Youth Policy Forum and Center on Education Policy (2001:12), it was during the late 1950s and early 1960s that the federal government entered the field of special education with various laws that supported development of captioned films for the hearing impaired, provided funds to train teachers of children with mental retardation, and authorized grants to states to educate children with disabilities. In the 1960s and early 1970s services to young children with disabilities became available through Head Start and other federal early childhood programmes. Head Start was a comprehensive programme designed to foster the healthy development of young children from low-income families. The programme has grown from a brief, eight-week summer programme for preschoolers in 1965 to a year-round programme today, serving children from birth to age five and pregnant women. Head Start provides children from low-income families with daily nutritious meals and many opportunities for social, emotional, and intellectual growth that can prepare them for success in school and in life. The programme also connects children to a health care source and provides vital support services to their families. The unique characteristic of the programme was that it admitted children with disabilities as well.

These initiatives, however, did not prove enough, as many as one million children with disabilities were excluded from school, and hundreds of thousands were in state run institutions (ibid). Special education underwent a dramatic evolution in mid-1970s with the passage of the Education for All Handicapped Children Act (Public Law 94-142) in 1975. By the late 1970s and early 1980s, those students considered more mildly or moderately disabled began to be integrated into regular class placements on at least a part-time basis. In 1986, the Office of Special Education and Rehabilitation Services launched the "Regular Education Initiative" that advocated the integration of general and special education into one educational system for all students. The regular education initiative was based on the premise that children with mild disabilities should be viewed as the shared responsibility of all the educators rather than as sole responsibility of special educators (Will, 1986). Sailor (1991) described it as one step closer to inclusive schooling than mainstreaming because the focus on adapting the general education setting to nurture and support students with mild disabilities. However, it differed from complete inclusion because it failed to address the education needs of children with severe disabilities. It was in the early 1990s when the international developments on inclusive education like the World Conference on Education for All, educators, parents and legislators continued to question the segregated system of schooling for the children with disabilities. The ensuing legislations have been directed towards achieving education of all learners in appropriate environments.

The United States was steadily progressing towards including all its children with disabilities into the regular educational system. The reauthorization of the Education for All Handicapped Children Act had been a significant step towards providing inclusive education in America. The Act was renamed as the Individuals with Disabilities Education Act. The Individuals with Disabilities Education Act (IDEA) provided funds to states for the education of children with disabilities. It contained detailed requirements for the receipt of these funds, including the core requirement of the provision of a free appropriate public education (FAPE). IDEA was comprehensively revised in 1997 by P.L. 105-17, but the federal government has continued to grapple with issues relating to the Act.

Provisions of IDEA

IDEA authorizes both federal funding for special education and related services and, for states that accept these funds, sets out principles under which special education and related services are to be provided. The requirements are detailed, especially when the regulatory interpretations are considered. The major principles include requiring that:

1. States and school districts make available a free appropriate public education (FAPE) to all children

with disabilities, generally between the ages of 3 and 21; States and school districts identify, locate, and evaluate all children with disabilities, regardless of the severity of their disability, to determine which children are eligible for special education and related services;

2. It requires children with disabilities to be educated in the "least restrictive environment". This would vary depending upon the needs of the child, but for most of the students with disabilities it would mean being served in regular education classrooms.
3. Each child receiving services has an individual education programme (IEP) spelling out the specific special education and related services to be provided to meet his or her needs; the parent must be a partner in planning and overseeing the child's special education and related services as a member of the IEP team;
4. "To the maximum extent appropriate," children with disabilities must be educated with children who are not disabled; and states and school districts provide procedural safeguards to children with disabilities and their parents, including a right to a due process hearing, the right to appeal to federal district court and, in some cases, the right to receive attorneys' fees.

IDEA helped fund special education and related services for about 6 million children with disabilities in school year 1998-99 (the most recent year for which data are published). The largest group of children served was those with specific learning disabilities. Other types of disabilities specified in the law are mental retardation, hearing impairments, speech or language impairments, visual impairments, serious emotional disturbance, orthopaedic impairments, autism, traumatic brain injury, and other health impairments (Apling & Jones, 2002).

The addition of learning disability as a disability category led to tremendous increase in the disability populations.

The term learning disabilities was first coined in 1963 by Samuel Kirk, but many other terms were used prior to this time to describe children with learning problems that are now termed as learning disabilities. Formulating a single definition of learning disabilities that is acceptable to all professionals in the field has proven difficult. As a result, several definitions are commonly utilized; these differ to some degree but generally have the same essential characteristics. The most commonly used definition first appeared in Public Law 94-142, the Education for All Handicapped Children Act (Federal Register, 1977). It was also a part of Public Law 101-476, the 1990 Individuals with Disabilities Education Act (IDEA) and is also a component of the 1997 Amendments to IDEA, Public Law 105-17 (Zecker, 2005).

The original Act has undergone many amendments since its inception. Some major amendments have been; expansion of the services to infants and toddlers with disabilities, required "transition planning" to better prepare for young people with disabilities for higher education, jobs and independent living and an emphasized focus on improving outcomes for children with disabilities. The 1997 amendments were most significant of them all and it facilitated the education of the children with disabilities. The changes included an added emphasis on results for students reduced the number of separately funded research, training, support programmes for students with disabilities and most importantly reduced the paperwork and procedural formalities associated with federal requirements.

The IDEA has been a major force in bringing about a noted progress in the way educational support and services are organized for children with disabilities. The IDEA promotes early intervention services in the natural environment of home and community settings in which children with disability participate. In recent years the infants and toddlers with disabilities are served within their homes, rather than in outside environments as outpatient, classrooms, nursery schools or hospitals. According to the American Youth Policy Forum & Centre on Education Policy Report (2001), more than half of the infants and toddlers with disabilities in the federal early intervention programme are being served at home.

Another recent initiative which has contributed significantly in the area of education for children with disabilities is the No Child Left Behind (NCLB) Act. The Act was signed by President George W. Bush in January 2002. This law, intended to raise academic standards and improve student achievement, has significantly influenced schooling, including approaches for educating students with disabilities. The law addresses four critical areas (Friend 2005):

- *Accountability for results:* All students are assessed yearly in grades 3 through 8 and once in high school to determine their progress and achievement, and the results of these efforts must be reported publicly.
- *Budget flexibility:* Up to 50 per cent of the federal funds for some education programmes (but not funds allocated for IDEA) may be blended. This provision has given more discretionary powers to state and local school officials for maximizing student achievement.
- *Options for student success:* In high poverty areas, the students are given an option to take the transfer to a school which is producing supposedly better results. In addition, students in these schools are entitled to tutoring, summer school and other programmes to improve achievement.
- *Research based teaching methods:* One important NCLB goal is that every child be reading by the end of third grade. This part of the law which is called "Reading First", funds scientifically proven methods of reading programmes.

The most important feature of NCLB to facilitate education of children with disabilities was accountability. In particular the NCLB requires every school to make adequate yearly progress towards the goal of achieving 100 per cent student proficiency in reading and mathematics by the year 2014. As one could fathom that this new Act is strongly influencing educators' thinking about raising expectations for students with disabilities, ensuring that these students access the same curriculum as other students implementing inclusive practices (Friend & Bursuck, 2005).

The educational provisions for children with disabilities were discussed in a chronological sequence to indicate that how the American society has moved from segregationist policies to one which upholds inclusion and equal opportunities to all its learners. Some other educational reforms which have contributed towards raising educational standards for children with disabilities are discussed below.

Other Educational Reforms

In the United States, two specific reforms have received widespread acclaim. Both reforms report low costs (US$30 per student in the second reform). The first, Robert Slavin's Success for All School Reform, which is a comprehensive reform model for elementary and middle schools. A comprehensive reform model is a programme to restructure what schools do, including curriculum, instruction, and professional development, accommodations for children who are having difficulties, school organization and everything that goes into making a school effective. It begins with two essential principles: prevention and immediate intensive intervention in 1st, 2nd, and 3rd grades of primary school. Critical components of the reform include: reading tutors (one-on-one instruction); heterogeneous age-grouped 90 minute daily reading group instruction; a family support team that provides parenting education to support children, and continuous/intensive teacher training. Every effort is made to address all students' learning problems within the context of the regular classroom. SEN students are fully integrated with tutoring support. Students with more serious disabilities receive in-class assistance from aides (trained para-professionals) and special education teachers. Research results report strongly positive effects in terms of grade-level growth in academic achievement (R.E. Slavin, in Lipsky & Gartner, 1997:382).

The second reform programme, Accelerated Schools Project (ASP), has been adopted by over 1000 primary and "middle" schools in 41 states since its inception in 1986. Learning is accelerated and enriched, rather than remediate and watered-down. The hallmark of Accelerated Schools is high expectations, an enriched curriculum that accelerates learning, and high level of parental involvement. The ASP is a whole school reform model that builds on capacities of teachers and schools through generalized training in a research-based problem-solving process. Used extensively in schools with large numbers of SEN and "at-risk" students (many of whom come from families at poverty levels), evaluations of the programme have shown substantial gains in student achievement, increased attendance, reductions in suspensions, and few grade repetitions (Peters, 2004).

As the chapter trailed through the history of educating children with disabilities in America, it attempted to show how special education has evolved on the basis of many factors. When education for children with disabilities started, its growth was unfathomable. Today, comprehensive services in a wide variety of settings are available to all age-groups of children through enactment of legislations and launching of programmes. This trend has been established surely to continue till it achieves the ultimate objective of including all its students with disabilities in the mainstream. However, there is always the other side of the picture. There is an ongoing controversy surrounding

IDEA funding concerns whether the federal government is living up to its "promise to fully fund" IDEA. There is little doubt that the nation has met some of the objectives of the IDEA but in the area of funding the federal government has not lived up to its commitment to cover substantial portion of the extra costs of carrying out the IDEA requirements.

Other than the incomplete financial support from the government there are other grave concerns like identification of children with disabilities. From the inception of IDEA, the federal government has been concerned about both the over-identification (that is, identifying children as disabled who are not) and the under-identification of children with disabilities (that is, failing to identify and serve children with disabilities). Concern about under-identification can be seen, for example, in the extensive "child find" requirements of the Act. Concern about over-identification is exemplified in the Act by recent changes in the state and substate formulas to remove possible financial incentives to over-identify and by extensive requirements for judging who is eligible for special education and related services (Apling and Jones, 2002).

There is yet another concern facing the federal government regarding the misidentification of children with disabilities. The AYPF and CEP (2001) had reported that African American students are referred to special education at higher rates than their share of the overall population. The over-representation of the African American students is especially dramatic among children identified as mentally retarded or emotionally disturbed. This misidentification results in negative effects on the child and also leads to resources being spent on non-deserving child.

These were some of the challenges that the federal government had been facing for implementation of IDEA. The realization of objectives set by legislation is indeed a daunting task. The earlier version of the IDEA enacted in

1975 required states and schools to carry out certain responsibilities and roles which had to be attempted first time. It also required them to contribute significant resources of their own to this effort. There is a constant struggle with competing pressures and complex issues for producing positive outcomes. Nonetheless, the nation has fared well and there is hope for the world to witness some outstanding achievements in the field of education for children with disabilities. The chapter shall now attempt a similar investigation for the United Kingdom so as to bring the two countries on a comparable platform.

Education of Children with Disabilities in United Kingdom

Some early contributions in field of educating children with special needs came from three European physicians, Itard, Senguin and Gugenbuhl. Jean Marc Itard (1774-1838) undertook the task of imparting language, self help and socialization skills to a moderately retarded child, named Victor who was captured at the forest of Aveyron at the age of twelve years. His behaviour was similar to animals and he lacked communication skills. Though Itard trained Victor considerably, his aim of making the boy reach normalcy was not accomplished. Itard's education consisted of individualized instruction, programming of learning experiences and immediate reinforcement. Senguin (1812-1880), Itard's student carried his task of educating the moderately retarded children forward. The difference however was that he did not concentrate on a single individual, he established first public residential facility in France. His Physiological Method (1907) was based on the belief that the blocked or damaged nervous system of the retarded could be reeducated to normalcy by motor and sensory training. He developed extensive didactic material for use by teachers. He advocated for gross motor movements followed by finer movements, leading on to perceptual motor exercises. He used colours, music and other devices to motivate the child. His training procedures relied heavily on Imitation. Johann J. Guggenbuhl founded a residential institution for the mentally challenged at Adenberg in 1841. He like Itard and Senguin, believed that a combination of medicinal and educational therapy could help to restore normalcy in habilitating his patients. Though he did not achieve success in completely remediating retardation, his sense training exercises were creative and remarkable, usage of Chinese gongs and phosphorus pencils in darkened rooms to establish and focus attention.

During the eighteenth century the first public schools for the deaf and the blind respectively were opened, followed in the early nineteenth century by the development of asylums for 'idiots'. Throughout this historical period children with special educational needs, for the most part, were unacceptable to the society (Wall, 2003). Till the end of the nineteenth century custodial care was considered best for the mentally challenged. It was because the general attitude of the community towards the children with disability was unfavourable.

In 1870, Forster's Education Act provided education for all children which laid the foundation of a positive thought system. In 1890s, Local Education Authorities (LEAs) were required to make special provision for all blind and deaf children and were given the option to provide for 'mentally defective' children. The Education Act 1944 instigated an appointment of a Minister of Education and the formation of the Ministry of Education, and stated that LEAs 'should have regard to the need for securing that provision is made for pupils who suffer from any disability of mind or body by providing special education treatment' (ibid:5). The Handicapped Pupils and School Health Regulations of 1945 identified 11 categories of disability: blind, partially blind, deaf, partially deaf, delicate, diabetic, educational subnormal, epileptic, maladjusted, physically handicapped and with speech defects. At this stage the medical practitioners undertook diagnosis and categorised the children so that they could receive education in appropriate setting. Such placing of children in fitting institutions led to many children being sent to boarding schools. By the 1950s parents revolted against this medial supremacy which separated their children from them rendering them even more vulnerable.

In 1970 Education (Handicapped Children) Act (DES, 1970) placed the responsibility of special needs provision within the remit of LEAs and as a result, special schools were created for children with moderately learning difficulties (MLD), severe learning difficulties (SLD) and severely subnormal difficulties (SSD). In 1978, in Britain, the Warnock Committee Report, a landmark in the history of education in the UK, listed essential provisions for children under five, and included children with disabilities as one of its top three priorities. The Warnock Committee distinguished between three forms of integration: locational, that is special units or classes in an ordinary school or a special school on the same site as an ordinary school; social, where locational integration exists but social interchange also takes place between special and normal; and functional integration, which involves special children joining their normal peers in regular classes on a full or part-time basis (Warnock, 1978 cited in Alur, 2002). Figures reported in the Warnock Report in 1978 suggested that around 20 per cent of pupils in schools would need, sometime during their schooling, some form of extra provision to meet their special educational needs.

The ensuing Education Act of 1981 upheld the key principles of the Warnock Report and placed a formal and mandatory emphasis on education of children with disabilities. The key points included (Wall, 2003):

- LEAs were given the responsibility of identification and assessment of special educational needs.

- Multidisciplinary assessments could lead to formal assessment of special educational needs, culminating in a statement of special educational needs, which would be reviewed annually.
- Focus to be placed on individual needs rather than categories of need.
- Provision for children with special educational needs to become the responsibility of the LEA.
- All categories of handicap were removed.
- Effective parental partnerships should be established.
- Integration should occur wherever practicable.

The current practice for working with children with special educational needs is guided by several key documents. These include the legislation contained in 1981 and 1996 Education Acts which embodied the philosophy of the Warnock Report; the 1988 Education Act which provided the framework for National Curriculum Guidance; the Code of Practice for SEN which has provided the most extensive guidance till date; and the expectations set out in the OFSTED documentation on Frameworks for Inspection (OSFTED, 1993 cited in Stakes & Hornby, 2000).

Much of the recent legislation for special needs education in England has been enabling, participatory and progressive. Since 1997, the government has embraced the concept of inclusion in many aspects of social policy. In education, the Office for Standards in Education (OFSTED) which inspects and judges schools on the extent to which they are inclusive of pupils with special educational needs (SEN) and the recent anti-discrimination legislation the Special Educational Needs and Disability Act (SENDA, 2001) has strengthened the right to a mainstream school place for children with disabilities. In addition, other initiatives such as the Department for Education and Skills (DfES) guidance Inclusive Schooling: Children with Special Educational Needs (DfES, 2001a), the revised Special

Educational Needs Code of Practice (DfES, 2001b), Removing Barriers to Achievement (DfES, 2004) and Every Child Matters (DfES, 2003), together provide a firm legislative context for further developments in inclusive education nationally. It would seem, therefore, that the government's strategy for SEN, demonstrates a commitment to inclusive education as a model for meeting special needs (cited in Rouse & Florian, 2006).

A glance at some of these provisions in detail would explicate the stance of the government towards facilitating the education of children with special needs.

Inclusion

The most vital issue concerning the education of the children with disabilities is their inclusion in the regular educational system. This has been upheld and advocated by the 1976 Education Act, reaffirmed by the 1981 Education Act which was based on the recommendations of the Warnock Committee Report of 1978. The Green Paper (DfEE, 1997) takes a more forthright stance on inclusion clearly stating that the government supports the Salamanca Statement on Special Needs Education and upholds the principle of inclusive education for all its learners unless there are compelling reasons to do otherwise. It further states that in cases where regular education is not possible for a child with disability, the special schools and units would provide for the special needs of the child.

National Curriculum

The National Curriculum is a prescriptive programme which determines the majority of curriculum content for all children up to the age of sixteen. Children with a wide variety and severity of SEN are therefore to be provided within this context. According to Stakes and Hornby (2000:3), "Some children with SEN will have little difficulty in keeping pace with their peers while for others this will be a problem. For many children with SEN their curriculum programme will have to take into account not only their pace of learning but also the level they can cope with".

All maintained schools and local education authorities must have regard to the National Curriculum 2000 which incorporates a statement on inclusion: providing effective opportunities for all children. This states that in planning and teaching the National Curriculum teachers have responsibility for: setting suitable learning challenges; responding to pupils' diverse learning needs; and overcoming potential barriers to learning and assessment for individuals and groups of pupils. The general and subject guidelines on planning, teaching and assessing the curriculum for pupils with learning difficulties, produced by The Qualifications and Curriculum Authority (QCA) help schools and others differentiate the curriculum. The NC was introduced to secure an educational entitlement for all pupils. It has a statutory inclusion statement that sets out the principles that teachers must follow to ensure that every child, irrespective of their abilities.

Office for Standards in Education (OFSTED)

Within the OFSTED inspection scheme, under which all the registered providers are inspected, there is an expectation that all providers should be able to demonstrate their commitment to parental partnerships and to SEN policies. OFSTED inspections focus on a range of issues regarding children with SEN; the quality of pupil learning, assessment of pupils, recording and reporting, curriculum, pupil's welfare and guidance and links with parents.

Code of Practice

The Code of Practice is described as 'a guide for schools and LEAs about the practical help they can give to pupils with special educational needs' (DfEE 1994:11). It makes recommendations as to how school might encourage the development of good practice in both the organisation of provision for children with SEN and the delivery of the curriculum for them. According to Stakes and Hornby (2000:5), "The Code sets outs a staged approach to meeting SEN, detailing the requirements for all involved in schools. It includes the responsibilities of all who work in schools, the governing body, and those with responsibilities for pupils with SEN in the LEA. The Code details procedures for identifying, assessing and planning programmes to address pupil's SEN."

Statement of Special Educational Needs

It is a legally binding document detailing the required educational provision for the pupil as well as the difficulties which the child has. It is determined by the recommendations of interested parties, with contributions from the school, the child's parents, representatives from the local services such as the school psychological service and social services; as well as representations from the LEA (Stakes & Hornby, 2000). These statements are reviewed annually to take into account the child's changing needs and circumstances.

A government programme which has made a significant difference to education of all children is called Every Child Matters: Change for Children. It is a cross-Government programme to deliver changes to the whole system of children's services - locally and nationally. The programme aims to enable local communities, schools and other children's services to work together more effectively to improve outcomes for all children and young people, with a particular focus on those at greatest disadvantage and including those who are disabled (Action Plan 1, UK Government, 2006).

The programme aims to deliver the following policy priorities which are specifically targeted at disabled children and young people.

- Delivery of the statutory frameworks for SEN under the Education Act, 2006 and for assessing young people in post-16 education with learning difficulties and disabilities (LDD) under section 140 of the Learning and Skills Act, 2000.
- Support for early years settings and schools to deliver the new Disability Equality Duty through the provision of guidance and the identification of a disability dataset that can be used across children's services.
- Action to improve outcomes and life chances of disabled children and young people through the development of effective and accessible services. This work is being informed by a joint review by HM Treasury and Department for Education and Skills of services for disabled children and their families and will feed into the Comprehensive Spending Review, 2007.
- Delivery, with Department of Health, of a comprehensive Child and Adolescent Mental Health (CAMH) Service, with effective multi-agency working between CAMH professionals and other health, care and educational services.

The government in order to support the outcomes of this programme had started the national grant programme in September 2005 to fund the voluntary organisations to do work of national significance. The grant programme was created to help the DfES make its funding to voluntary organisations more strategic and to make it easier for organisations to apply for funding for work that improves outcomes for children, young people and families. It aims to contribute to increasing stability in the voluntary and community sector by offering longer term funding. The programme is open to charities, or non-profit-making organisations set up and run on similar lines to a charity. A limited number of strategic and project grants will be awarded in the programme's second round. The total fund value is known to be £ 3,300,000 (governmentfunding. org.uk 2007).

A noteworthy change in the policy documents is that the students with disabilities are being made part of the regular education system. The recent programmes and policies are meant to be for all children and the fact is specified within the document itself. The present trend in education for children with disabilities is towards inclusive practices, but implementing instructional practices to support them requires an understanding of their importance and commitment to their realization. The chapter has highlighted progression of educational trends for children with disabilities in two countries. Both the countries have shown similarities in the way educational services are being designed for the inhabiting population of children with disabilities through the enacted legislations and programmes. It is, therefore, motivating to go on with a comparative analysis for making clear distinctions and recording similarities.

A Comparative Analysis

Historical Progression

It is interesting to note the nature of competing policy and programme frameworks for children with disabilities in USA and UK. The two countries have moved progressively ahead maintaining a similar pace towards policy and programmatic changes for the education of the children with disabilities. The early attempts to cater to the special educational needs began with residential schools for the blind and deaf students. The efforts originated in the Europe during the eighteenth century, rapidly growing in the nineteenth century. Special schools for those with mobility impairments came later around the turn of the twentieth century. North America followed a similar route, although beginning later than in Europe. At the same time, those with intellectual impairments were largely institutionalized as uneducable in both Europe and North America. Disability was conceptualized more as a matter of tragedy striking an individual and service in any form to children and persons with disabilities was considered a matter of charity. Disability was considered a medical condition as opposed to the current definitions which regard it as a social state. Hence medical intervention for disability was regarded appropriate. The prevalent medical model delegated supreme powers to the medical professionals who were trained to diagnose, treat and cure illnesses, and not to alleviate social conditions or circumstances. Second World War and its aftermath witnessed the emergence of family, community and consumer models of service delivery for SEN students. The social model began to be developed and parents pressured for deinstitutionalization in both Europe (e.g., the concept of normalization promoted by Wolfensberger) and in North America (e.g. the landmark decision of Brown *vs.* the Board of Education 1954 in the US where the Supreme Court established that school segregation denies students equal educational opportunity).

Legislations

The legislations concerning the education of the children with disabilities were promulgated around the same time (Table 5.2). It is vital to record that many of the legislations were positively influenced by the international covenants. Like most countries in the world the United Kingdom and United States of America support the Salamanca Statement. The statement drawn up by a UNESCO World Conference, held in Salamanca (Spain in 1994) called upon all Governments to "adopt as a matter of law or policy the principle of inclusive education, enrolling all children in regular schools, unless there are compelling reasons for doing otherwise".

Table 5.2: A comparative display of legislations concerning education of the children with disabilities in UK and USA.

International Influences	United Kingdom	United States of America
	Education (Handicapped Children) Act, 1970 The Education Act, 1976 The Education Act, 1981	Education of the Handicapped Act (EHA), 1970 Education for All Handicapped Children Act, 1975 Education of the Handicapped Act Amendments of 1983 Education of the Handicapped Act Amendments of 1986.
World Conference on Education for All 1990 Salamanca Statement, UNESCO 1995	The Education Act, 1993 The Education Act 1996	Individuals with Disabilities Education Act (IDEA) 1990 Individuals with Disabilities Education Act Amendments of 1997.
DAKAR Framework, (Education for all) UNESCO 2000	The Disability Discrimination Act, 1995 The Special Educational Needs and Disability Act 2001 (SENDA) The Education and Inspections Act 2006	Americans with Disabilities Act, 1990 No Child Left Behind Act (NCLB), 2001. Individuals with Disabilities Education Improvement Act 2004 (still referred by acronym IDEA)

All the recent legislations in both countries support inclusion of children with disabilities in the regular educational system and have described the role of local education authorities, teachers, and parents.

Early Identification and Inclusion Statistics

The two countries have done a commendable work in the area of early identification and service to the children with disabilities. It has been well established that like all other children, children with disabilities benefit a great deal from early intervention, in the absence of which they might develop secondary disabilities. The interesting fact is that vast majority of these identified children are in the educational mainstream.

In US, three decades ago, an estimated 1.75 million children with disabilities received no educational service. A large number of students with disabilities were never identified or incorrectly diagnosed. It has been estimated that the number of children served under the IDEA has increased by about 75 per cent in just over two decades (AYPF and CEP, 2001:16).

As far as inclusion of children with disabilities is concerned, United States has reported an exponential growth. During 1994-95 the number of school districts reporting Inclusive Education programmes in US has tripled. (Gartner & Lipsky, 1997:100). It is estimated that three-quarters of students with disabilities in the age-group 6-11 years are being educated in regular education classrooms with non-disabled children for a significant part of the day (AYPF & CEP, 2001:20). Even the infants, toddlers and young children are receiving early intervention and preschool services (ibid: 22). This has largely been made possible through two IDEA programmes; the Part C programme for infants and toddlers ages 0 through 2, and the Preschool Grants programme for children ages 3 through 5. The Part C programme offers funding for infants with developmental delays or other disabilities for providing early intervention services which include education, therapeutic, and social services, as well as family training and support, special technological devices, and more. The Pre-school grants programme provides free and appropriate education to all children with disabilities within the 3 to 5 age-group.

In UK there are approximately 1.4 million pupils with SEN were identified in the United Kingdom in 2002-03. If an education authority or board believes that it should determine the education for a child with SEN, it must draw up a formal statement of those needs and the action it intends to take to meet them. Almost 300,000 pupils had these statements (called a Record of Needs in Scotland). In England, the number of pupils with statements of SEN increased from around 195,000 in 1994 to a peak of nearly 260,000 in 2001.

Table 5.3 indicates that almost 250 thousand pupils in schools in England had a SEN statement in January 1999. The percentage of pupils with statements has continued to climb from 2.6 per cent in 1995 and 2.9 per cent in 1998 to 3.0 per cent in 1999. The proportion with a statement varied by type of school, from 2.5 per cent in maintained secondary schools to 0.9 per cent in maintained nursery schools. The proportion of pupils in special schools and pupil referral units with a statement of SEN was 94 per cent and 23 per cent respectively.

The Education Act, 1981 and the Education Act 1993 placed a qualified duty on local education authorities in England and Wales to ensure that children with a SEN should have their needs met wherever possible in mainstream schools. In Scotland, education authorities are also encouraged to integrate children with a SEN into mainstream schools wherever possible. In January 1999, 60 per cent of all pupils in England with statements of SEN were in maintained mainstream schools (nursery, primary and secondary), compared with 54 per cent in 1995. The percentage of all pupils with SEN statements who were placed in special schools (maintained and non-maintained) or pupil referral units (PRUs) fell to 38 per cent in 1999 from 44 per cent in 1995.

Table 5.3 : Pupils with statements of Special Educational Needs (SEN): By type of school[1]

(Thousands)

England	Maintained mainstream	Special Schools and Pupil Referral Units	Independent
1994	100.6	88.5	5.5
1995	113.2	92.3	5.8
1996	127.3	94.3	5.8
1997	134.1	94.0	6.5
1998	141.4	94.4	6.5
1999	147.6	93.6	6.9
2000	152.8	93.3	6.8
2001	158.0	93.7	6.6
2002	149.9	92.1	7.0
2003	150.9	92.6	7.0

1. Pupil referral units did not exist prior to 1995. Estimates were made for 2001 because the SEN data were known to be incomplete.

Source : Department for Education and Skills. www.statistics.gov.uk/STATBASE/Expodata/Spreadsheets/D7298.csv

These figures indicate the achievement of the two countries in the field of inclusive education. The figures are alibi to the sustained efforts and dedication of the two countries towards mainstreaming the children with disabilities.

Educational Programmes

The programmes for education in both the countries involving children with disabilities exhibit a great deal of similarity as well. For instance, the federal programme Head Start served as an inspiration for the UK government programme named Sure Start. The latter was launched in 1999 to bring together early education, childcare, health and family support for the benefit of young children living in disadvantaged areas and their parents as opposed to Head Start which existed since 1965. It is however noteworthy that Head Start's incarnate, Early Head Start was designed in 1994 to provide high-quality child and family development services to low-income pregnant women and families with infants and toddlers. The major work focus of Sure Start is to ensure delivery of; free education for all aged 3-4, affordable and quality child care and after-school activities in all areas, and children's centres and health and family support in disadvantaged areas. The Head Start delivers comprehensive and high quality services designed to foster healthy development in low-income children and guarantee and delegate agencies that provide a range of individualized services in the areas of education and early childhood development; medical, dental, and mental health; nutrition; and parent involvement. Both the programmes are working towards poverty alleviation through their efforts in providing for emotional, social, health, nutritional, and psychological needs of the children in low-income families. (See Table 5.4 for detailed comparison of the two programmes)

The Challenges

Despite the early initiatives and support legislations and programmes the two countries are facing numerous challenges in implementing the inclusive education proposal to its fullest. Here are some challenges which have been identified by internal agencies which could be termed comparable. Apart from some culture specific issues it is evident that challenges faced by the two countries involve areas of curriculum, accessibility, parental involvement, over-identification, professional development, and costs and funding.

OFSTED (2004) has identified a number of continuing challenges to achieving better outcomes for children with special educational needs (SEN) and disabled children in United Kingdom including: delays in identifying children's needs and in putting appropriate interventions in place; wide variations in provision leading to a postcode lottery

Table 5.4 : Comparison of Head Start and Sure Start (Hong Kong Council of Social Service 2004)

	UK Sure Start	**USA Head Start**
Objectives	To achieve better outcomes for children, parents and communities by : - increasing availability of childcare for all children - improving health and emotional development for young children - supporting parents as parents and in their aspiration towards employment To halve children poverty in 2010	- increasing the school readiness of young children in low-income families - help break the cycle of poverty by providing preschool children of low-income families with a comprehensive programme to meet their emotional, social, health, nutritional, and psychological needs
Targets	Families from pregnancy until their children are 14 (16 for special need children)	Children from birth to age 5, pregnant women, and their families
Responsible parties	Sure Start Unit of the Children, Young People and Families Directorate, report to Department of Education and Skills and Department of Work and Pensions	Administered by the Head Start Bureau, the Administration on Children, Youth and Families, Administration for Children and Families, Department of Health and Human Services
Local administrating bodies	Local authorities, primary care trust, jobcentre plus, local communities and NGOs	The programme is locally administered by community-based non-profit organizations and school systems

Contd...

Table 5.4 : *(contd...)*

	UK Sure Start	USA Head Start
Major work focus	ensure delivery of : - free education for all aged 3-4 (12.5 hours of free "educare" support per week for aged 3-4) - affordable and quality child care and after-school activities in all areas - children's centers and health and family support in disadvantage areas	- deliver comprehensive and high quality services designed to foster healthy development in low-income children. - grantee and delegate agencies provide a range of individualized services in the areas of education and early childhood development; medical, dental, and mental health; nutrition; and parent involvement Early Head Start programmes are designed to produce outcomes in four domains: * Children's development (including health, resiliency, social competence, and cognitive and language development); * Family development (including parenting and relationships with children, the home environment and family functioning, family health, parent involvement, and economic self-sufficiency); * Staff development (including professional development and relationships with parents); and

Contd...

Table 5.4 : *(contd...)*

	UK Sure Start	**USA Head Start**
		* Community development (including enhanced child care quality, community collaboration, and integration of services to support families with young children).
Scope of service	Sure Start services bring together universal, free, early education and more and better childcare, with greater support where there is greater need through children's tax credit, children's centres and Sure Start local programmes. Sure Start services include: " Childminding and Home Childcarers " Children's centres " Children's Information Service " Early Excellence Centres " Extended schools " Funding " Health and family support " Neighbourhood Nurseries " Out of School " Sure Start local programmes	*Programme Services Areas* *Disabilities* : Fully including children with disabilities in Head Start program. *Education* : Ensuring children enrolled in Head Start begin school ready to learn *Family and Community Partnerships* : recognize the vital contributions made by parents and community members. Health : health screenings evaluate the child's overall health status and regular health check-ups and good practices in oral health, hygiene, nutrition, personal care and safety Programme Management and *Operation* : focus on delivering high-quality child development services to children from low-income families.

contd...

Table 5.4 : *(contd...)*

	UK Sure Start	USA Head Start
	" Maintained Nursery Schools " Strengthening Families	
Existing provision	In 2004, there are 524 Sure Start local programmes, helping up to 400,000 children living in disadvantaged areas Besides, there are1,139 neighbourhood nurseries, 207 early excellence Centres and 67 Children's Centres (one-stop service that provide childcare, education, health, employment and parenting support)	In 2004, there are about 47,000 Head Start classrooms and 19,200 Head Start centres
Programme evaluation	Two levels of evaluation, both national and local The national evaluation of the Sure Start programme is a long-term, wide ranging study designed to evaluate the efficacy and cost-effectiveness of Sure Start. The first phase of the national evaluation runs from 2001 to 2008 All Sure Start local programmes are required to undertake an evaluation of their programme. This will assist in understanding how services are performing and inform the ongoing development of each programme	National Head Start Impact Study

Contd...

Table 5. 4: *(contd...)*

	UK Sure Start	**USA Head Start**
Performance standards / outcome measurement	Public Service Agreement Targets by 2006 - 12 per cent reduction in the proportion of young children living in households where no-one is working - increase in the proportion of children having normal levels of communication, language and literacy at the end of the Foundation Stage - increase in the proportion of young children with satisfactory speech and development at age 2 years - increase in the proportion of babies and young children aged 0-5 with normal levels of personal, social and emotional development for their age - 5 per cent reduction in the proportion of mothers who continue to smoke during pregnancy	All Head Start programs must adhere to Programme Performance Standards
Government expenditure / Unit cost	£499 million (03-04) for about 400,000 children aged under 4, i.e. about £1,248 per child	$6,774,848,000 (2004) US $7,092 per child

and a lack of parental confidence in the system to meet children's needs; children who could be taught in mainstream schools being turned away because schools are inaccessible or staff feel ill-equipped to meet their needs; children in mainstream schools not receiving a curriculum appropriate to their needs and not playing a full part in the life of their school; and special schools feeling uncertain of their future role within a policy of inclusion.

The challenges facing the education of children with disabilities in USA are quite similar to the ones experienced in United Kingdom. The AYPF and CEP (2001) have identified ten major challenges:

1. The access of students with disabilities to the general curriculum, academic courses and general assessments must be increased.
2. Academic achievements of students with disabilities must be improved.
3. There is a need to address the over-representation of African-American students in special education. It is important address these culturally relevant issues for reducing inappropriate referral and placements in special education.
4. Ensuring that more students with disabilities graduate from high school.
5. Encouraging more students with disabilities to prepare for, enroll in, and complete higher education.
6. To prepare more students with disabilities for jobs.
7. To increase the supply and improve the skills of all teachers working with students with disabilities.
8. Review and reduce IDEA paperwork and procedural requirements which are producing unintended consequences for the children with disabilities like the paperwork takes time away from important teaching

responsibilities, it is also a significant factor affecting the decision of the special education teachers to leave the profession.

9. Bridging the "digital divide" for students with disabilities which will require funding investments, professional development, wider dissemination of research about integrating technologies into special education services and consideration of students with disabilities in all federal, state, and local technology plans and programmes.
10. Challenges remain in areas such as parental involvement, over-identification of children with disabilities, costs and data collection.

The two countries have spearheaded the cause of inclusive education in the world through their policies and programmes and have succeeded in giving an equal status to their population with differential abilities. The challenges are just an evidence of policy being implemented and would surely and soon be overcome to pave way to a just world.

Conclusion

The chapter in an attempt to review the educational policies and programmes related to children with disability in the representative high income countries has unfolded various issues regarding education of children with disabilities. These issues offer insights into the way the educational system must respond to the diverse learning group. At the governmental level, certain adequate steps need to be taken to ensure inclusive education practices for children with disabilities. First and foremost there is a need to have a comprehensive data on all children with disabilities so that policy and programmes could be effectively developed. Secondly, effectual evaluation and monitoring systems must be in place for the current educational programmes. At the school level, the most important role of the parents and teachers is identification of children who may display difficulties in learning. It is the first step towards finding out whether a child has special educational needs or not. The special educational needs of the children must be met as far as possible in a regular school. It is however not possible until one responds to child in terms of changes in the curriculum, pedagogy, professional development of the staff, external resources, technological assistance and parental involvement.

The consequence of the World Conference on Education for All: Meeting Basic Learning Needs 1990 has been radically positive for the disadvantaged group of children. It has dauntingly challenged exclusion from education making it a political agenda in many countries. This has helped to focus attention on a much broader range of children who may be excluded from or marginalized within education systems because of their apparent difficulties. These may include those who are already enrolled in education but for a variety of reasons do not achieve adequately, those who are not enrolled in schools but who could participate if schools were more flexible in their responses, and the relatively small group of children with more severe impairments who may have a need for some form of additional support. The results have been significant and far-fetched in the United States of America and United Kingdom, which have matched up to the international expectations in terms of educating their populace comprising children with disabilities. The two countries have set examples for the rest of the world especially the low and middle income countries for making adequate educational provisions for the children with disabilities in order to make them financially and socially independent citizens who contribute to the country's economy.

Education systems respond in most high-income countries by offering a dual-track approach to students with disabilities. Those who can thrive in general education programmes are encouraged to do so. Those who are unable to be in general education have the option to choose specially designed instruction or other assisted learning programmes and an array of related services (e.g. psychological and counselling services, language, speech and hearing, guidance, social work, transportation, physical and occupational therapy, and medical services required for diagnosis or evaluation). These services and opportunities vary considerably, even across high-income countries. According to a OECD Report (2003), children with disabilities who are in receipt of additional resources are being educated - special schools, special classes in regular schools, or regular classes. In some countries, e.g. Spain, the United States, Italy and Canada (New Brunswick) make extensive use of regular classes while others prefer to use special schools, e.g. Belgium (Flemish Community), the Czech Republic, Germany and the Netherlands. Some countries make extensive use of special classes in regular schools, e.g. France, Finland and Japan.

Financing and support of educational services for students with special needs is a primary concern for all countries, regardless of available resources. Yet, a growing body of research asserts that IE is not only cost-efficient, but also cost-effective, and that "equity is the way to excellence" (Skrtic, 1991). If the two nations buckle down to the work ahead with the same energy and sense of purpose that has characterized the past two decades, the world can look forward to another era of impressive progress in special education and a brighter future for children with disabilities.

References

Action Plan 1, UK Government. Retrieved from http://www.dfes.gov.uk/publications/des/docs/DES%20Action%20Plans.doc on 24th April 2007.

Alur, Mithu (2002). Introduction, in Seamus Hegarty and Mithu Alur (Eds), *Education and Children with Special Needs: From Segregation to Inclusion*, New Delhi: Sage Publications.

Apling, Richard & Jones, Nancy Lee (2002), *The Individuals with Disabilities Education Act (IDEA): Overview of Major Provisions.* Retrieved from http://usinfo.state.gov/usa/infousa/educ/files/ideaover.pdf on 18th March 2007

American Youth Policy Forum (AYPF) and Center on Education Policy (CEP) (2001). Twenty Five Years of Educating Children with Disabilities: The Good News and the Work Ahead. Washington DC: Author.

Australian Institute of Health and Welfare (AIHW) 2004. *Children with disabilities in Australia.* AIHW cat. no. DIS 38. Canberra: AIHW.

Clark, C., Dyson, A., Millward, A. & Robson, S. (1999) Theories of inclusion, theories of schools: Deconstructing and reconstructing the 'inclusive school', *British Educational Research Journal*, 25(2), 157-177.

Dakar Framework of Action (2000). UNESCO.

Department for Education and Employment (DfEE) (1994). *Code of Practice on the Identification and Assessment of Special Educational Needs.* London:HMSO.

Department for Education and Employment (DfEE) (1997). *Excellence for All: Meeting Special Educational Needs.* London: Stationery Office.

Friend, Marilyn (2005). *Special Education: Contemporary Perspectives for School Professionals*, Idea 2004. Boston: Allyn & Bacon.

Friend, Marilyn and William D. Bursuck (2005). *Including Students with Special Needs: A Practical Guide for Classroom Teachers* (IVth Edition). Boston: Allyn and Bacon.

governmentfunding.org.uk 2007 Retrieved from http://www.governmentfunding.org.uk/VCSSearch.aspx?WCI=htmSchemeView&WCU=DSCODE=DSCLIVEGF,SCHEMEID=12-S74,SEARCH=DS=DSCLIVEGF on 21st April 2007

Hong Kong Council of Social Service (2004). Retrieved from http://www.ispcan.org/documents/vid/HeadStart-HongKong.doc on 30th April 2007.

Lipsky, D. K. & Gartner A. (1997). *Inclusion and School Reform: Transforming America's Classrooms.* Paul Brookes Publishing Co., Baltimore.

Inclusive Education at Work: *Students with Disabilities in Mainstream Schools*, OECD, Paris, 1999.

Metts, Rober L. (2000). *Disability issues, trends and recommendations for the World Bank.* World Bank.

Organisation for Economic Co-operation and Development (OECD) (2003). *Education Policy Analysis, Diversity, Inclusion and Equity: Insights from Special Needs Provision*, Paris: OECD.

OFSTED (2004). *Special Educational Needs and Disability: Towards Inclusive Schools.* Author.

Osgood, R. (2005). *The History of Inclusion in the United States.* Washington, DC: Gallaudet University Press. 226 pages.

Peters, Susan (2003). *Education Notes (Education for All: Including Children with Disabilities).* Education Notes Series: World Bank. Retrieved from http://siteresources.worldbank.org/EDUCATION/Resources/Education-Notes/EdNotesDisability.pdf on 2nd April 2007.

Peters, Susan (2004). *Inclusive Education: An EFA Strategy for All Children.* World Bank.

Rouse, Martyn and Lani Florian (2006). Inclusion and achievement: student achievement in secondary schools with higher and lower proportions of pupils designated as having special educational needs *International Journal of Inclusive Education,* Vol. 10, No. 6, November 2006, pp. 481-493.

Sailor, W. (1991). Special education in the restructured school. *Remedial and Special Education*, 12(6), 8-22.

Seguin, E. (1907). *Idiocy and its Treatment by the Physiological Method.* Columbia University.

Skrtic, T.M. (1991). The special education paradox: equity as the way to excellence. *Harvard Educational Review*, 61(2), pp. 148-206.

Stakes, Richard and Gary Hornby (2000). *Meeting Special Needs in Mainstream Schools: A Practical Guide for Teachers* (second edition). London: David Fulton Publishers.

UNESCO (1994). *The Salamanca Statement and Framework for Action on Special Needs Education.* World Conference on Special Needs Education: Access and Quality, Salamanca, Spain, 7-10 June 1994. Paris: UNESCO.

Wall, Kate (2003). *Special Needs in Early Years: A Practitioner's Guide.* London: Paul Chapman Publishing.

Will, M. (1986). *Educating children with learning problems: A shared responsibility*. Washington DC: Office of Special Education and Rehabilitative Service, US Department of Education.

Zecker, Steven G. (2005). Underachievement and Learning Disabilities in Children Who Are Gifted. *LDA of Oregon Newsletter, Fall 2005.* Retreived from http://www.ldaor.org/Newsletter-Fall2005.html on 7th April 2007.

SUMMARY

This work is a product of a continuous and consistent effort of the authors towards developing a holistic understanding of the child with disability as part of the larger ecological systems which constantly influence and interact with each other. It has offered insights on various themes related to development and education of children with disabilities. The aim of exploring the theoretical areas related to the education of children with disabilities has been fulfilled to a great extent. This book has endeavoured to encompass the historical and current perspectives for all the selected chapters.

Each chapter raised its own issues and has contributed to the learning. The knowledge gained through this work is difficult to be summarized in few words. Nonetheless, the authors would endeavour to state some key learning which happened during the course of formalizing this book. Primarily the authors would affirm what has been stated almost in every chapter that children with disabilities are children first. They have similar aspirations, desires and needs as their normally developing peers. Our country has not been able to righteously respond to their needs which have resulted in their invisibility and helplessness. The physical and attitudinal barriers, segregation in form of special schools for any and every kind of disability and non-implementation of the existing policies are some of the major reasons for their social isolation.

The book involved exploration and complete understanding of the international covenants and country legislations and provisions. It helped in developing a social and legal perspective on inclusion. Inclusion of children with disability in the normal social activities is their human right. Since, children with disabilities have long experienced stigma and discrimination it might take them little long to organize power and fight for their rights in our country's context. However, it may not be a distant reality as the activism has begun in the West for equal rights and opportunities.

INDEX

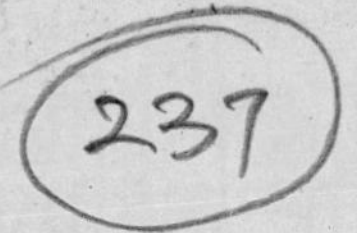